Beadweaving
MASTERY

Beadweaving MASTERY

More than 15 Beading Projects for Jewelry and Accessories

Heather Laithwaite

Author's acknowledgments

How do I say thank you to those who helped me so much? This book would not have been written if it was not for them. I have found this experience to be both exciting and overwhelming.

To Tanya Olivier, my friend, student and right hand – thank you for all the support you have given me, and trying out all my patterns. I know how many hours it all took. Thank you for holding me up at times when I needed it. Thank you for giving me your work for the book.

To my students whose work is in this book – thank you for believing in me, for pushing me to explore new boundaries, and for all the encouragement you gave me. I value your support.

To Tina, my daughter, thank you for pushing me forward and for being so enthusiastic about the beads. Thank you, too, for the criticism, because I knew when I had a winner. Thank you for believing in me so utterly, and for your enthusiasm for creating. We make a good team.

To Mark, my youngest son, thank you for so often helping me out with advice, and with the computer when I got stuck. Thank you for the sheer delight you show in my work.

To Kevin, my eldest son – it has been a busy year, yet you still found time to set me up with the computer. Thank you for letting me phone you whenever I needed advice, and for teaching me the steps I needed to know. I am very grateful.

To Graeme, what can I say? For holding my hand when I got so tired, for cooking so many dinners in the last month, for giving me the space that I needed to write this book, and for sourcing the things that I needed …
Thank you, my love.

To Wilsia, my publisher, thank you for the opportunity in letting me express myself through my beads, and for all the help you have provided. It has been a delightful whirlwind.

To Ivan, my photographer, thank you for all the input. I enjoyed it, and your patience. And to Nicky, my illustrator, thanks for your very hard work and enthusiasm and for going the extra mile. What a small world it is!

www.fwmedia.com

17   16   15   14   13   5   4   3   2   1

DISTRIBUTED IN CANADA BY FRASER DIRECT
100 Armstrong Avenue
Georgetown, ON, Canada L7G 5S4
Tel: (905) 877-4411

DISTRIBUTED IN THE U.K. AND EUROPE BY F&W
MEDIA INTERNATIONAL
Brunel House, Newton Abbot, Devon, TQ12 4PU,
England
Tel: (+44) 1626 323200, Fax: (+44) 1626 323319
Email: enquiries@fwmedia.com

DISTRIBUTED IN AUSTRALIA BY CAPRICORN LINK
P.O. Box 704, S. Windsor NSW, 2756 Australia
Tel: (02) 4560 1600, Fax: (02) 4577 5288
E-mail: books@capricornlink.com.au

SRN: U8139
ISBN-13: 978-1-4402-3875-8

Everything you need for most projects is available in kit form from heather@laithwaite.net.

A mail order catalogue is available from Heather Laithwaite
PO Box 42
Plumstead 7801
South Africa

Originally published by Metz Press
1 Cameronians Avenue
Welgemoed, 7530
South Africa

Copyright © Metz Press 2013
Text copyright © Heather Laithwaite
Photographs copyright © Metz Press

PUBLISHER AND EDITOR	Wilsia Metz
DESIGN AND LAY-OUT	Lindie Metz
COVER DESIGN	Geoffrey Raker
PHOTOGRAPHER	Ivan Naudé
COPY EDITOR	Nikki Metz
ILLUSTRATOR	Nicky Miles
REPRODUCTION	Cape Imaging Bureau
PRINTING AND BINDING	Printed and bound in China by WKT Co Ltd

Contents

Introduction

"Very little is needed to make a happy life "
Marcus Aurelius – Roman philosopher

Beads have a fascinating history, seemingly as old as that of mankind. Beads have been used for many different reasons, but by far the most prevalent use is for the adornment of the human body, to decorate various articles of clothing, and for religious connotations.

The word bead comes from the Old English word *bede*, which means *prayer*. Prayer beads have been used in many religious traditions, for example the Rosary of the Roman Catholic faith. Several other religions have beads strung in a special way and used by their members during acts of worship and meditation.

Another fascinating aspect of beads is that various items of jewellery have been used to identify different ethnic and cultural groups within countries and continents – especially in Africa.

Owing to their beauty and overall appeal, beads have also been synonymous with trade, and had been accepted as a standard form of currency and barter for many centuries.

BONE AND STONE

The first beads, associated with Neanderthal Man, were discovered at La Quina in France and dated back to nearly 38 000 BC. Large quantities of beads dating back to 10 000 BC were found in the Upper Palaeolithic sites of Europe and Russia. In those times beads were worn to signify prowess in hunting, for spiritual assistance and protection, as well as for self-beautification. The beads were worn in amulet bags worn around the neck or waist.

The earliest beads were made from animal bones and teeth, or consisted of animal vertebrae and horns stringed together to make pendants and adornments. Sea shells and colourful seeds and berries were also commonly used. Stones, perforated with bow drills, were used in the Indus Valley during the Neolithic Period, while coloured coral and shells were made into netted beadwork worn as armbands, belts and other regalia in the South Pacific around 1 000 BC.

In North America the American Indians developed beadwork long before the Europeans introduced manufactured beads. In prehistoric times the Indians made their beads from copper, turquoise and quartz, as well as seeds and sea shells. Early American Indian craft workers often used porcupine quills for their intricate beadwork.

CLAY AND GLASS

Although many different peoples have used and developed beads throughout the history of mankind, the art of beadwork embroidery is credited to the ancient Egyptians. Clay and faience beads (ceramic quartz fired with different coloured oxides or glazes) – the forerunners of glass beads – were first made by the ancient Egyptians around 4 000 BC. Ancient Egyptian wall paintings often display figures wearing multi-coloured collars of faience beads. These were also the first beads to be produced in large quantities for what was even then an ever-expanding market.

Glass was invented in Mesopotamia or Egypt around 2 000 BC and glass beads were among the first mass-produced items manufactured specifically for trade purposes. Small glass seed-beads are produced by making long, fine hollow cylinders which are cut into short sections and the ends smoothed. This technique was first developed in India in 200 BC. Glass seed-beads were first traded with Arabs along the African trade routes to Zanzibar, Tanzania, Kenya and the island of Lamu between AD 200 and 1500. Their popularity grew and they soon became one of the most demanded items of trade. Over the next 1 500 years seed beads from India were traded as far afield as Malaysia, Sumatra and Vietnam.

Knowledge of Indian seed-bead manufacture spread initially to Sri Lanka and then on to Sumatra, Thailand, Vietnam and Malaysia. These became

known as Indo-Pacific beads and became one of the most successful trade items of all time during the period 200 BC to the 16th century.

Until the 15th century the supply of beads was controlled by the wealthy trading nations – the Islamic world, India and China. But by the end of the 15th century explorers such as Bartholomew Diaz, Vasco Da Gama and Columbus had opened the trade routes and by the 17th century the Portuguese, Spanish, French, British and Dutch had colonised most of the New World. World trade was now dominated by Europe and a large variety of beads became available from factories all over Europe.

The Venetians

In the 9th century monks from the Benedictine order were tasked with the making of glass tiles needed for intricate mosaic work in churches and palaces of the time. Their glass-making skills were passed on to the Venetians who were the leading European glassmakers until the 20th century. The glassmakers of that time jealously guarded the secrets of their trade and glass workers who moved out of their areas were considered traitors and were thus often killed.

Towards the end of the 13th century the Venetian glass workshops were moved to the island of Murano – the seclusion of this island keeping artisans and their skills confined and protected. There, bead-making began at the start of the 14th century with drawn glass-beads (margarite) mass-produced from 1490. These small glass beads became a major trade item in Asia, Africa and America, used by traders, explorers and missionaries to barter, to trade and even to entice people to come to church. During the 16th and 17th centuries, margarite beads were used extensively by dressmakers to adorn garments. Authorities eventually banned this practice, considered extravagant, and restricted the use of these beads to the adornment of hair ornaments.

By the 16th century Italian bead-making factories were threatening the Indian markets and for the next 300 years the Venetians were the dominant world producer of beads. By the end of the 19th century other European countries have caught up, however, which forced the Venetian bead factories to amalgamate – a strategy that protected them to the middle of the 20th century when they were no longer able to compete with the Bohemians.

Bohemian glass beads

Bohemian glass-beads also date back to the 9th century but it was not until the 17th century that France, Germany and Bohemia became significant producers of glass seed-beads. By the middle of the 20th century Bohemia (today part of the Czech Republic) became the leading European producer of glass seed-beads. After the Second World War the communist government of Czechoslovakia consolidated all the family businesses

that produced beads and created one modern, well-equipped factory in Zasada where seed beads were produced on a large scale. In addition, moulded glass-beads were produced at Ornela.

After the collapse of communism in 1989 small family businesses have again been formed and the industry continues to thrive to this day. Also after the Second World War, many skilled German bead-makers left Czechoslovakia and settled in Germany and Austria establishing bead-manufacturing factories there. Another country specialising in seed beads today is France. The Chaudemanche factory in Lyons produces beads in highly unusual colours that have worldwide appeal.

BEADS FROM ASIA AND THE EAST

Some of the oldest bead manufacturing centres are found in Asia and the East, where the seed-bead market is dominated by India and Japan. In Firozabad, India, hollow glass-beads used for garment decoration, have been produced since 1960. These beads were imported from Bohemia before. A Czechoslovakian couple introduced furnace-wound beads and lamp-wound beads to Varanusi, India, in the late 1930s. These are now made in Purdalpur while seed beads have been produced in Varanusi since 1981 using machinery imported from Japan. Today thousands of Indian women are employed manually stringing beads for export purposes.

Japan is a large bead manufacturer – famous for the excellent, high quality Miyuki Delicas beads. Glass seed-beads were first made in Japan in the 1930s, while mass production only commenced in 1949. The Delicas bead was developed in 1982 and is regarded as one of the most consistent high-quality bead available today.

How to use this book

I have written this book to read like a novel – start at the beginning with the simplest beading and progress through the stitches as they become more advanced. The Cleopatra necklace is a combination of all the techniques up to that point in the book and is an excellent consolidation.

To read a beading pattern, you need to know the following: The bead size is written as 9° or 6-mm, and the colours are referred to by symbols. For example 3C 11° means 3 seed beads in size 11 in colour C. A size indicated with the simbol ° always refers to seed beads, while other bead sizes are indicated in millimetres.

Each section has an introduction dealing with the general technique. This technique is then applied in specific projects where I often refer back to the general information. It is advisable to read through the entire text of a project before starting to work on it.

Have fun!

diamanté balls

Materials

It is a good idea to familiarise yourself with the materials used in beading, as choosing and using the right beads, threads, needles and tools often show in the final piece. But to get started you need just a small bag of beads, scissors, a needle and thread – and you can take them anywhere. Just remember, beading can become very addictive!

Beads

In this section I would like to give you an understanding of the different types of beads, of which there are many.

SIZING

The first thing you should become familiar with is the different sizes of beads, and how the sizing of beads works. The seed bead is so called because of its similarity in size and shape to that of an ordinary seed. Its sizing is typically written as 6° or 11°. This indicates how many beads of a particular size equal 0 – written 'ought'. Thus, size 11 means 11 beads are equal to 0 and size 6 means 6 beads are equal to 0 – and size 11 then obviously is the smaller bead. Seed beads most commonly come in sizes 6, 8, 9, 11, 14 and 15.

triangles

TYPE AND SHAPE

Apart from different sizes, seed beads also come in different types. The Japanese and Czech seed beads are very similar from a sizing perspective. The only real difference is that the inside holes of the Czech beads tend to be smaller and generally more uneven than those of the Japanese seed beads. Japanese seed beads, as mentioned before, are of a superior quality because the manufacturing equipment they use is much more modern and technologically advanced. Beads such as the Miyuki Delicas

pressed glass shapes

bugles (3 mm)

chip stone

daggers

are quite exquisite. Their shape is slightly different to that of other seed beads – being more like a fine tube chopped up than a rounded seed bead – and they also have larger holes. Working with Delicas beads is a particularly rewarding experience and the finished article has a texture which is hard to beat. The only downside is that Delicas beads are more expensive.

In addition to seed beads, there are also the Japanese hex beads. They follow the same sizing system and are made from fine six-sided tubes. They are longer in length than seed beads.

The bugle bead is made from the same fine tubes as seed beads, but it is not as small and is more tubular in shape. Again, the quality of the Japanese bugle is far superior to the Czech beads, which often have very rough edges that easily cut through thread – most distressing when all your hard work literally falls to pieces! If you do decide to use the Czech bugles, use a seed bead on either side of the bugle bead – this will prevent the thread from fraying and eventually breaking. Another tip whilst working with bugles is to keep some waterpaper handy – this will enable you to sand off any rough edges. The 7-mm bugle bead is the more commonly used size, but I personally prefer the smaller 3-mm bugle.

triangles

bugles (7 mm)

NEW DEVELOPMENTS TAKE ON SHAPE

The Japanese, being regarded as the leading innovators, are continually striving to keep their dominance in the delivery of quality beads to the world. One such development was the introduction of the Magatamas bead range. These are larger beads with an off-centre hole, which allows for the bead to hang as a teardrop. This style is also available in square beads, triangles and twisted hex.

The triangle bead is another great development from Japan. Some manufacturers have introduced a softly rounded triangle bead, while a bead with harder and more definite corners has been introduced by others. Both can be used to create the most amazing contemporary abstract beadwork. They are also ideal for use in peyote and brick stitch, and when making spiral ropes.

seed beads

cubes

drops (Magatamas)

Czech crystals

The round or shaped bead is measured in diameter and can be as big as 14 mm or as small as only 3 mm in diameter. I like to use these beads frequently.

COLOUR COORDINATION

When you start a beading project, first take all the beads that you have decided to use, put them together and make sure the colours complement each other. It may seem a simple task, but it actually does take practice and will allow you as a new beader to gain in colour confidence. Another helpful aid in selecting colours that blend well together is to look at the different colours in a particular fabric or print that appeals to you. Study these colours and observe the harmony between them. Home décor books often have examples of colour-coordinated rooms. Study these and improve your colour-matching skills. Don't forget to look towards nature as an excellent source of colour-combining inspiration!

materials

Start by choosing a main colour. Now see which colour is opposite your main colour on the colour wheel. This colour will really bring your main colour to life, making it more intense and alive, for example orange and blue, or purple and yellow. If these primary colours seem too loud and striking, you may feel more comfortable with something a little more toned down, for example sand and turquoise or damson and mustard. Again, using designed fabrics is a wonderful medium to gain experience regarding the relationship of colours to each other. Remember that colours used should be restful to the eye.

COLOUR WHEEL

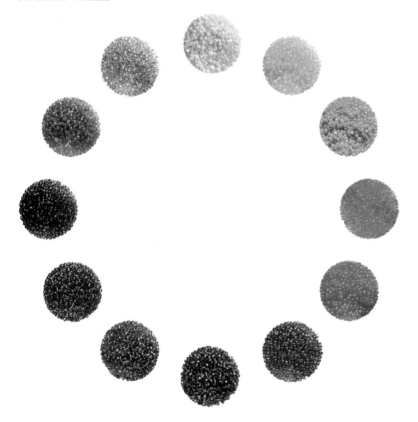

This colour wheel shows the primary, secondary and tertiary colours in delicate seed beads

FINISHES

Another aspect of colour when it comes to beads is the different finishes in which beads are available and the totally different effect and look each finish can create. There are transparent beads, sparkling beads, beads that are opaque, luster, matte, silver-lined, mother of pearl and nickel-plated – to name but a few.

A different effect will also be achieved by using thread of various colours – especially if you are using transparent and opaque beads.

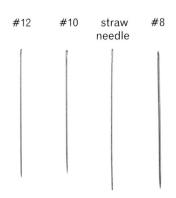

#12   #10   straw   #8
              needle

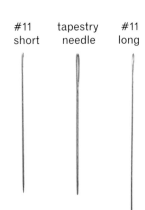

#11   tapestry   #11
short   needle   long

Needles

Beading needles come in several sizes (10, 11, 12, 13 and 15); the higher the number the smaller the needle. Most beading needles are approximately 3,5 – 5,5 cm in length, with sizes 10 to 12 being fairly flexible. A size 12 needle is the most common and versatile with 11 seed and smaller beads. If threading is difficult, use a tapestry size 28, and if a short needle is preferred use a quilting "betweens" needle. Having said that, it is always best to use a proper beading needle.

Threads

There is no one perfect thread and most beaders have their own ideas and opinions as to which brand or type is the best. Play around with different threads until you find one with which you feel the most comfortable.

Regardless of the type of thread used, it is important to match the colour of your thread to the colour of your beads. This is particularly so with the use of transparent beads, where, for example, a blue bead woven on gold thread will acquire a greenish cast.

Waxing of the threads to make them easier to work with can also be of a big help to many people. It strengthens the thread and reduces its tendency to knot.

The following is just a short summary of the different types of threads available and their respective advantages and disadvantages.

NYMO: originally developed as an upholstery thread, it is a bonded nylon non-twisted filament thread. It is sold on card bobbins in size OO (finest) to E (heaviest) and is available in a wide range of colours. This was one of the first threads readily available to beaders and at the time of writing this book is only now becoming available to us in South Africa. It is very strong, does not rot, and is unaffected by sunlight. However, it should always be stretched before use, and it does have a tendency to shred. I like Nymo and it is my personal favourite. It is strong and thin enough to go through a seed bead several times. Waxing is also a suggestion, though I don't find it necessary.

C-LON: a relatively new thread developed specifically for beading. It has the same properties as Nymo and is available on 80-yard bobbins in a rainbow of colours. Advantages and disadvantages are the same as for Nymo, except it does not need waxing and is less stretchy. It is comfortable to work with and strong and resilient, but a little heavier. It is not yet readily available.

SILAMIDE: developed for the clothing industry, this 2-ply twisted nylon thread with a round cross section is sold on 40-yard cards. It is immensely strong for its thickness and the twist holds the beads as you work. It is not as freely available as Nymo.

GEL SPUN POLYMER (GSP): was developed for the fishing industry and is made of lots of filaments braided and bonded together. This makes a very strong, fine line roughly half the thickness of a similar weight mono-filament. The two makes available are Berkley Fireline (only available in a smoke-grey colour) and Power Pro (only available in white and moss green). This thread has very good strength and body.

NYLON MONOFILAMENT: a very contentious thread! There are those beaders who love it and there are those who refuse to use it. The Madeira monofil has a finer thread in 60 and a heavier thread in 40. I particularly like the invisible finish that you can achieve with this thread. It's commonly called the invisible thread and I believe that its advantages far outweigh its disadvantages. On the upside it allows for the true colour of the bead to come through, it's easy to unpick your work and it is much easier to thread smaller beads. The thread also allows for the beads to fit snugly together. On the downside the thread has a tendency to knot and it can become difficult to see if you get caught up.

Tools of the Trade

You don't need a lot of special tools when you do off-loom beading, but some items wil make life easier.

MAGNIFIER LAMP

Light and magnification are extremely important with beading. Magnifier lamps come in table models or floor models.

SPRING-CLIP OPTICAID

These clip-on magnification glasses are essential for beaders who need a little assistance when doing finer and more detailed work. They fit most plastic and metal spectacles and come in three different lens strengths.

BEADING MAT

This is an inexpensive mat with a velvety feel, that enables the beader to effortlessly pick up and thread beads.

BEAD DISH

This is a plastic dish with several receptacles that can hold a variety of different coloured beads – a tray of sorts. This is my preferred receptacle, with the beading mat inside, holding my pots of beads.

PLIERS

Long-nosed, round-nosed, and flat-nosed pliers are all jewellery makers' tools that the beader will find very useful.

THREAD ZAPPER

This is a very handy little battery operated thread burner. It took me a little while to get used to it, but it is so useful that I hardly cut and trim thread with anything else anymore.

SURGICAL MEMOSTATS

These are forceps that lock under pressure and are used to hold thread or needles. They are extremely useful when you need to pull a needle through beads with small holes.

THREAD CUTTER

This is a round disc that you wear around your neck. It looks like a pendant and is very convenient for beading classes and travelling.

FASTENERS

There is a huge range of fasteners available at vastly differing prices. It's worth spending a little extra on a good quality fastener rather than spoil your hard work with a fastener that rusts and discolours.

Getting to know your beads

This project is intended to help you become better acquainted with the different bead sizes – it can be unnecessarily confusing in the beginning!

Debbie
Single-stranded necklace

For this project I used 3-mm, 6-mm, and 8-mm Gutermann round glass beads, which are measured in diameter. I have also used 6°, 11° and 14° seed beads, which are small round beads with a large centre hole. The Japanese bead is the best in terms of uniformity, and it has good sized hole in the middle. Remember, the higher the number of the bead, the smaller the bead size. A spacer is a silver, gold, nickel or brass bead, and in this case flat and disc-like in shape.

You will need
1 barrel clasp
46D 3-mm round beads
22A 6-mm round beads
18B 6-mm round beads
6C 8-mm round beads
10E 6° seed beads
168A 11° seed beads
190B 11° seed beads
12H 14° seed beads
Nymo thread in colour B
#11 beading needle
36 spacers (5-mm)

To travel means to work the thread back through 6 to 8 beads or more.

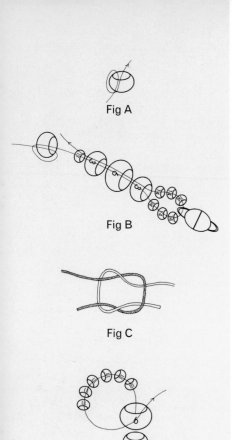

Fig A

Fig B

Fig C

Fig D

Fig E

Thread up with a long thread, about 2,5 m, and put on a stop bead – any temporary bead that you take your needle through twice, being careful not to split the thread (Fig A). Leave a tail of about 20 cm.

1 Pick up 1A 11°, 1D 3-mm , 1A 6-mm , another D 3-mm and 6H 14°. Now take the needle through the end loop of the barrel clasp and back through all the beads (3-mm, 6-mm, and 3-mm again, and the 11°A) back to the stop bead (Fig B). Tie a reef knot (Fig C) – left over right and right over left.

2 Now pick up 1D 3-mm, 1A 6-mm, 1 spacer, 1E 6°, 1 spacer, 1A 6-mm, 1D 3-mm, and 1B 6-mm. Make sure at this point that your tension is taught, and the beads all sit next to each other.

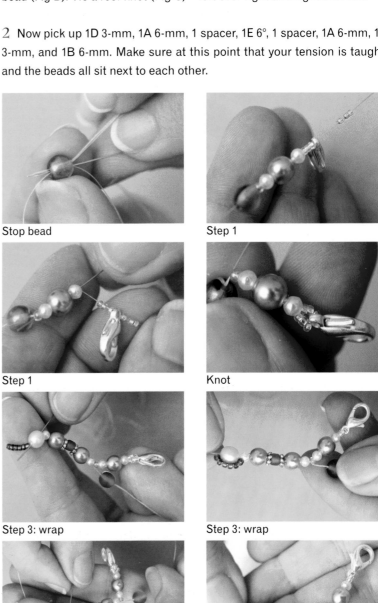

Stop bead

Step 1

Step 1

Knot

Step 3: wrap

Step 3: wrap

Step 3: wrap

Step 3: wrap

beads

3 Pick up 6A 11°, pushing your beads down to the top of the last bead. Wrap the beads down over the big bead, and needle up the centre – hold the tension. Pick up 6B 11°, and, pushing the beads to the top of the big bead, wrap again, needle up the centre. Continue from the beginning of Step 3 until you have 6 wraps in alternating colours. Spread evenly and keep taught (Fig D and E).

4 Pick up 1D 3-mm, 1A 6-mm, a spacer, 1B 6-mm, 1D 3-mm, 1A 6-mm, a spacer, 1D 3-mm , 1C 8-mm C, 1D 3-mm and a spacer, 1B 6-mm and 1D 3-mm.

5 Pick up 1B 6-mm and repeat Step 3, having 6 wraps.

6 Pick up 1D 3-mm, a spacer, 1B 6-mm, a spacer, 1D 3-mm, 1A 6-mm, 1D 3-mm, a spacer, 1E 6°, another spacer, 1C 8-mm, a spacer, 1E 6°, another spacer, 1D 3-mm, 1B 6-mm, and 1D 3-mm.

7 Pick up 1B 6-mm and repeat Step 3, having 6 wraps.

8 Pick up 1D 3-mm, 1A 6-mm, 1D 3-mm, 1A 6-mm, a spacer, 1E 6°, 1 spacer, 1A 6-mm, and 1D 3-mm.

9 Pick up 1B 6-mm and repeat Step 3, having 6 wraps.

10 Pick up 1D 3-mm, 1A 6-mm, a spacer, 1B 6-mm, 1D 3-mm, 1A 6-mm, a spacer, 1D 3-mm, 1C 8-mm, 1D 3-mm, a spacer, 1B 6-mm, 1D 3-mm, a spacer, 1E 6°, and a spacer, 1D 3-mm.

11 Pick up 1B 6-mm and repeat Step 3, having 8 wraps (half-way). Now repeat the other half, working Step 10, 9, 8, and so on backwards – replicating the first half.

12 Having threaded on the 6H 14°, take the needle through the loop of the other end of the barrel clasp, and back through the D 3-mm, and so on, all the way back to the wrapped bead. Go through one of the outside loops (or wraps), and then head back towards the barrel again, through the centre of the big bead, and all the beads once more, and through the 6H 14°. Now strengthen the entire neck piece by travelling all the way through the beads to the other end, taking up any slack if there is any. End where the tail was left, knot, and take each side in a different direction. Knot and dab with a little clear nail varnish. Travel and cut.

Tassels

Tassels or fringes are such fun to make and they have so many uses! They always look good, whether they are made with small delicate beads, or heavier and larger ones. When making tassels you will often find the ideal opportunity to add those few special beads you were saving to make a project your own, or simply to use up those odd beads you had lying around. Tassels can be used to adorn cupboards, or to put onto handbags and belts. They can also be attached to neckpieces, or worn as jewellery, and much, much more!

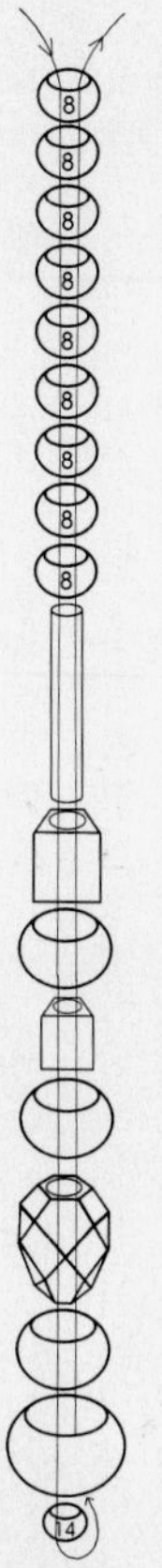

Method 1A

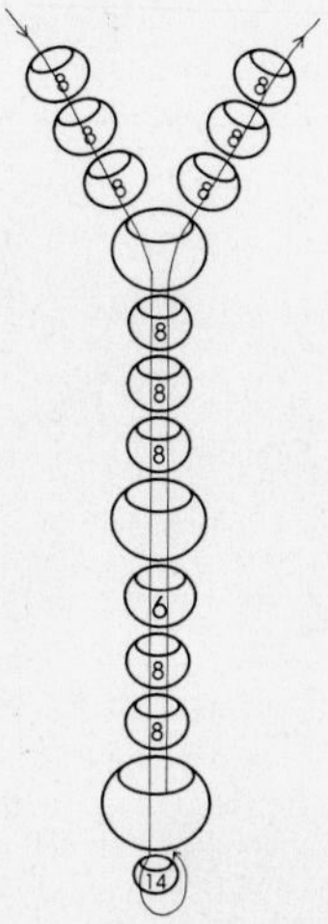

Starting at the top of a tassel, pick up a number beads, all the way to the bottom, finishing with a small bead.

Now take your needle and thread over the last bead and back through the next bead all the way to the top again (Fig A).

Method 1B

Follow the same method as above, but, having come back up, stop a few beads down to pick up the same number of beads, thus making a branch. Fasten off before starting a new tassel (Fig B).

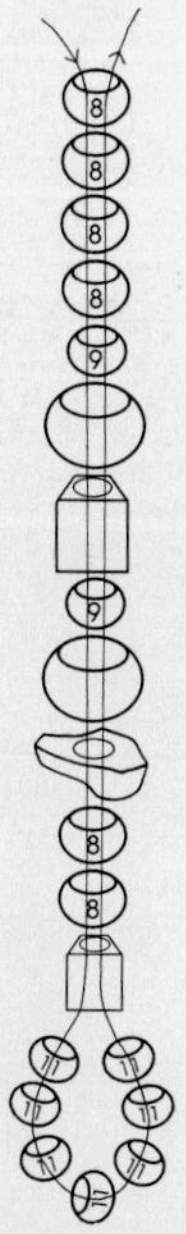

Method 2A

Starting at the top of the tassel, pick up a given number of beads, finishing with a bead with a good-sized hole. Now pick up 7 little beads and go back through the bead with the good-sized hole, thus making a loop. Take the needle back, through all the beads, to the top. This is a very useful method with which to fill out or bulk little beads (Fig C).

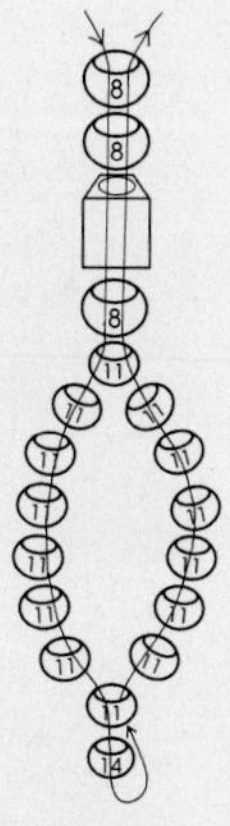

Method 2B

Follow the same method as above, but, having come out of the bead with the good-sized hole, pick up 9 beads. Now go back through the second bead from the needle, pick up a further 6 beads and go through the first bead after the bead with the good-sized hole.

You have made a little picot on the end, and still have the loop (Fig D).

Fig A

Fig B

Fig C

Fig D

Method 3A

Starting at the top of the tassel, pick up a number of beads, all the way to the bottom, finishing with a small bead. Take the needle over the last bead and back through the next bead and up a few more. Now make a picot: pick up 3 more beads and enter up into the next bead, travelling to the top (Fig E).

Repeat as often as you need, making little picots.

Method 3B

Follow the same method as above, but, having turned at the bottom, and up a few beads – this time you will make a branch. Pick up a few beads ending in a small one. Turn and go up into the next bead, travel up the entire branch and a few more up the main body. Repeat as often as need be, taking care not to pull too tight (Fig F).

Try playing with all these methods, change bead sizes, and see which methods you could possibly combine. Have fun!

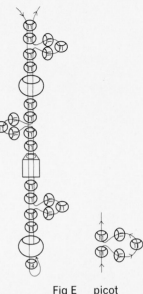

Fig E   picot

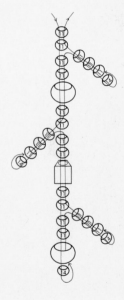

Fig F

Christina
Tassel fob, using Method 1A

In order for you to become familiar with the different kinds of beads, I have used a wide variety for making this tassel. What better way to learn than while having fun? It is important that you use a soft thread for this project – otherwise the tassels lose their fluidity. I like Nymo D; you could also use a strong nylon thread. If you don't have 9° seed beads, these can be substituted with 11° seed, whichever you have. Please make sure that the large bead you choose for the top (any shape or size) has a large enough hole for the cord to go through.

You will need

1 large bead (top focal point)
55A 9° seed beads, colour to match top
25B 9° seed beads
57C 9° seed beads, dominant colour
10D 7-mm bugle
14E 6° seed beads
20F 4-mm round beads, first colour
10G 3-mm bugles
12H 4-mm round beads, second colour
4I 6-mm rhombic
12J 6-mm round beads
12K 11° seed beads (turning bead)
4L large chips, first colour
4M large chips, second colour
15G 11° seed beads
large bead (10-mm) to put on top of focal bead if you wish
35 cm cord, fine enough to pass through bead
#11 beading needle, long
2 m Nymo D in matching colour

Fig A

Take your cord and, lying the thread side by side, very neatly wrap each end to stop it from fraying. Wrap about 5 or 6 times, end with a buttonhole stitch, take your needle back down through the centre, and cut. Having done both ends, join them to make a loop (Fig A). Tidy in the same way as above. Make sure the cord goes through the chosen bead. I use a piece of wire bent into a U-shape to take the cord up the bead (Fig B). Make sure your wrapping is neat and not too thick. Pull the cord up the bead until you have only the wrapping protruding from the bead (Fig C). This is what you will use to sew.

Fig B

Fig C

Thread your needle with 2 m of Nymo and fasten the thread into the wrapping on the end of your cord, just below your bead.

First tassel

1 Pick up 3A 9°, 2B 9°, 2C 9°, 2A 9°, 1D 7-mm bugle, 1E 6°

2 Pick up 3C 9°, 1F 4-mm round, 1G 3-mm bugle, 1G 11°, 1H 4-mm round; 1I rhombic, 1F 4-mm round, 1J 6-mm round, 1K 11°

Having put on the last little bead, take all the beads up to the top, next to your cord. Pass the needle over the last little bead and up the 2nd bead, next to your last bead, and all the way to the top as in Method 1A. Make sure it is lying snug against the cord. Take your needle through the cord, and start the next tassel, working round the cord to fill in 8 tassels.

Second tassel

3 Pick up as in Step 1, then pick up 4C 9°, 1F 4-mm round, 1G 11°, 1G 3-mm bugle, 1B 9°, 1H 4-mm round, 1L chip, 1C 9°, 1H 4-mm round, 1A 9°, 1F 4-mm round, 1J 6-mm round, 1K 11°

Take the beads to the top of your thread, and finish your second tassel. Secure the second tassel into the cord, and start the third leg.

Third tassel

4 Pick up as in Step 1, then pick up 3C 9°, 1A 9°, 2C 9°, 1F 4-mm round, 1G 11°, 1G 3-mm bugle, 1G 11°, 2A 9°, 1M chip, 1F 4-mm round, 1E 6°, 1H 4-mm round, 1J 6-mm round, 1K 11°

Take the beads to the top of your thread and finish the third leg. Secure the third tassel into the cord, and start the next leg.

Having made the tassels around the circumference of the cord end, make another one on the inside of the cord.

Your tassel is made up of 8 legs, so repeat Step 1 plus Step 2, Step 1 plus Step 3, and Step 1 plus Step 4 – making six tassels. Then choose any two to repeat again to make 8 legs.

Having finished the last leg, open up the base, and stitch through a few times, making sure all is very secure, knotting in-between. Cut very close to the wrap. Dab a little clear glue or clear nail varnish to the base. Put a little more glue or nail varnish next to the top, on the beads. Pull the cord so that the legs lie close to the master bead. Leave to dry. Once dry you can put another bead on top of the master bead to finish it off if you so wish.

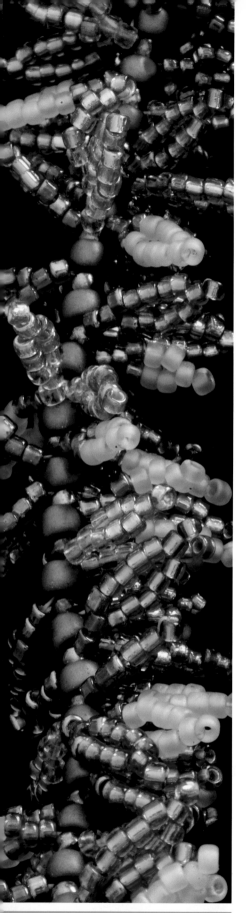

Cali
Tassel bracelet, using Method 2B

This bracelet is made up of 11°, 8° and 6° seed beads. It's a great project for using up some of those leftover colours – as long as the base colour is there. I have used six colours in this bracelet, but you may add more, or use less.

You will need
35G 8° seed beads
34H 6° seed beads
210A 11° seed beads
384B 11° seed beads
192C 11° seed beads
368D 11° seed beads
328E 11° seed beads
504F 11° seed beads
6-mm round bead
7 m Nymo-D thread
#11 beading needle, long

Thread onto your needle 2,5 m of Nymo-D thread. Add a stop bead by twice going through 1G 8° (Fig A). Leave a tail of about 20 cm.
Now pick up as follows:

1 1G 8°, 1H 6°, and repeat until it is long enough to almost meet around your wrist (I used 31G 8° and 30H 6°). Start and end with 1G 8°. Now make the end-button bead. Thread on 2A 11°, the 6-mm round bead, followed by 1A 11°. Now take your needle over the last bead and back through the 6-mm round bead, the 2A 11°, and the first G8° on the main body of the bracelet. Make sure there is no slack, and start your first tassel (Fig B).

For the tassels I have used six colours: two colours to a tassel, and three different tassel colours.

TASSEL COLOURS   3A + 6B and then 4B + 1A
3C + 6D and then 4D + 1C
3E + 6F and then 4F + 1E

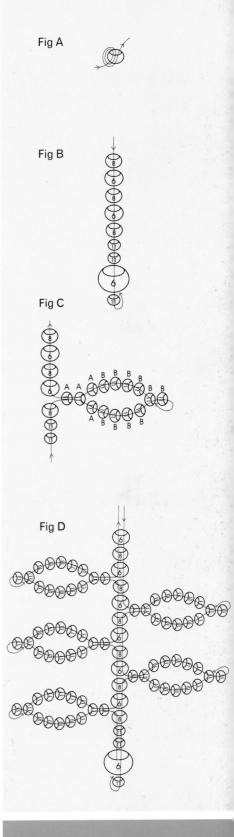

Fig A

Fig B

Fig C

Fig D

Step 1

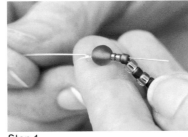

Step 1

Tassel – Fig C

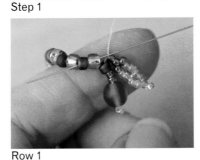

Row 1

Row 1– Fig D

Loop for end-button

Row 2

Row 2

Row 1

1 Pick up 3A and 6B, and make the little picot on the end by moving the beads up the thread, snug. Then take the thread through the second B from the needle, needle pointing towards the base and pick up 4B and 1A; pass the needle through the last 2A beads next to the base, needle pointing towards the base (Fig C). You have completed your first tassel.

Continue through the next H 6° and G 8° on the base, and start the next tassel in 3C and 6D as in Step 1, then make the 3rd tassel in E and F. After each tassel go though H 6° and G 8°, using the three different combinations all the way to the end (Fig D).

   Having made the last tassel, and gone through the last G 8°, make sure the stop bead is not loose. Snug up, and make the fastening loop. Pick up 15A, and go back through the first two A beads you picked up next to the main body on your loop. Make sure the loop fits the button bead. Snug up and undo the stop bead. Knot the tail with a reef knot and make sure there is just a little movement. Don't let it come apart! At this point, use the tail to strengthen the loop by going through the beads, and tie again with the working thread. Go back to the working thread and go through the G 8° and H 6°.

Row 2

Continue the sequence of tassels all the way back to the other end, having two tassels at the same points after H 6° all the way. Continue through the 2A 11° on the button end and through the 6-mm round bead into the A11°. Turn, go back through the 6-mm round bead, and so on, back to G 8° and lastly H 6°, and start the next sequence. From the H 6°, the tassel is shorter.

Row 3

TASSEL COLOURS   3A + 4B and then 2B + 1A
                 3C + 4D and then 2C + 1D
                 3E + 4F and then 2E + 1F

If the bracelet is a little loose on the wrist, make another loop 4 or 5 beads in from the first loop, and when fastening put both loops over the button, one acting as a safety loop.

2 Pick up 3A + 4B, go back through the second B from the needle, and then pick up 2B + 1A, and through the last two A beads, continue towards the loop end. Go through the loop to strengthen, and through the first G 8°, now heading towards the button, and continue for …

Row 4

You complete the second sequence working as for Row 3.

Row 5

TASSEL COLOURS   3E + 3F and then 1E + 1F

3 I have chosen only one tassel to bring out the colour. Make the whole row in the one tassel working towards the loop end. Make a tassel at the loop to fill in the space, and another at the button. Your bracelet should be nice and full. End off by taking the thread down the entire base beads and then knotting and travelling. If, however, you feel like going back and adding a few tassels, or a few bigger beads as in the bracelet on the photograph below, you are more than welcome!

A new thread

If your thread becomes a little short, travel up the tassel ahead and back down. Knot at the base of the tassel and leave the thread (to mark the place). Take the new thread and go back 4 beads on the base and through 2, knot. Now go up and down a tassel and come out where you left off, continue. The old thread has still to be worked away, by travelling and knotting, travel again and cut. Do the same with the tail of the thread you put in.

The spiral rope

The spiral rope is one of my favourite pieces. You can dress it up or down, or break it up – the combinations are endless. I have mixed colour with the small beads, and then broken it up with the larger beads. I also used the magnetic bead just to have some more scope and versatility.

With the rope there are two components, the core and then the spiral. The core runs up the middle, and the spirals are built up with beads running up the outside of the core. The basic recipe is the core, with three beads making up the spirals running up the outside.

Use a long thread, because the fewer joins the stronger your piece of work. I find 2,5 m of thread a comfortable length with which to work.

Fig A

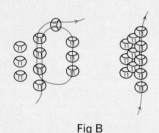

Fig B

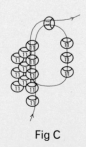

Fig C

Method 1

STEP 1: Thread on 4 beads in the first colour (these beads are the core beads) and 3 beads in the second colour (these beads make up the outer spiral). Leave a tail of about 20 cm (always leave enough thread to be able to work with) and take the needle back through the 4 first colour beads, from tail to top (Fig A), snug up. Push the spiral to the left, keeping the core to the right.

STEP 2: Pick up 1 more in your first colour plus 3 beads in the second colour. Push all the beads down the thread to meet up with the existing beads. Needle up from tail to top of 3 of the first colour plus the new bead, equals 4 beads (Fig B). There should be 1 first colour bead not used at the base of the first colour run. Again push the spiral to the left, to sit on top of the first spiral, leaving the core on the right. It is important to make sure that the spirals sit neatly **on top** of each other.

STEP 3: Pick up 1 more in your first colour plus 3 in the second colour. Continue as in the previous step. There will be 2 first colour beads not used at the base of the first colour run (Fig C). Continue building your rope to the desired length. The core grows one bead each round.

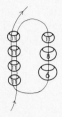

Fig A

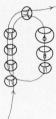

Fig B

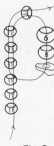

Fig C

Method 2

This method is the same as the first, but the size and the type of beads are varied, giving the spiral a much more textured look. Here I have kept the size of the beads in the core all the same, and added the texture to the spiral only, but you could vary the core in just the same way (Fig A, B, C).

To begin a new thread

Never let your thread become too short to be manageable. It is better to waste a little bit of thread than to have to struggle with the ending.

To begin a new thread mid-spiral, knot after having added the outer spiral beads – your thread should be coming out of the core. Knot onto the thread at the base of the nearest spiral, and leave (Fig D). This will also be a marker as to where the join is, which is to be strengthened at a later stage.

Thread up with new thread and make sure you have a good length (I find 2,5 m to be a comfortable length), because every join can be a week point, so the fewer joins the better.

Go back up the core heading towards the beginning, entering about 4 beads in from the place you had to join, and travel another 4 beads up to the start in the core. Turn down the nearest spiral and knot at the base of the spiral. Travel to where you left off, picking up one core plus … continue as normal. Go back and tidy up both threads, travelling up the core, and knot into the nearest spiral, one in either direction. Travel and cut. Carefully dab a spot of clear nail varnish on the last knot.

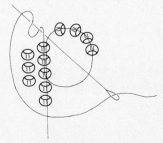

Fig D (French knot)

Lisa

Spiral rope lariat, magnetic beads
Method 1

The lariat (a long rope) can be worn around the neck – the magnetic beads catching the rope together down the middle. It can also be wrapped around the neck once and caught in the centre, or you can wear it around your wrist. I have used 11° seed beads for the spiral, but you could also use 9°.

You will need

225A 11° dark seed beads
180B 11° medium seed beads
180C 11° light seed beads
180D 11° medium-light seed beads
305E 11° contrast seed beads (core bead)
32F 6° seed beads
30 matching 6-mm round beads
16 magnetic facetted pillar beads (5 x 8 mm)
12 m Nymo D-thread
#11 beading needle, long

Thread up with about 2,5 m of thread.
The first section is worked in only the 11° see beads:

1 Pick up 4E, 3A, and then go through the 4E beads again from the tail up. Push the A beads to the left. These are the spiral beads. Leave the core beads on the right (Fig A, B).

2 Pick up 1E, 3B, and push the beads to the end of the thread next to your work. Needle up the 3E core beads on the rope and the new core bead to make 4E core beads. Push the new spiral to the left, to lie on top of the A beads in spiral 1 (Fig C, D).

3 Pick up 1E, 3C, and push the beads down the thread, and needle up the 3E core on the rope and the new core bead to make 4E core beads. Push the C spiral to the left to lie on top of the B and A spiral (Fig E).

4 Pick up 1E, 3D, and push the beads down the thread, and needle up the 3E core beads on the rope and the new one to make 4E core beads. Push the D spiral to the left on top of C, B, A.

5 Pick up 1E, 3A, and push the beads down the thread, and needle up the 3E core beads on the rope and the new one to make 4E core beads. Push the A spiral to the left, on top of D, C, B, A.

Fig A
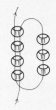

Fig B

Fig C

Fig D

Fig E
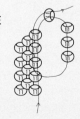

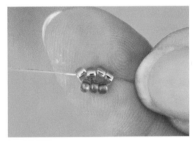

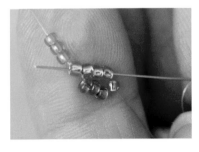
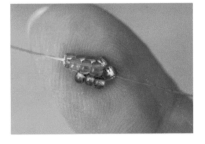

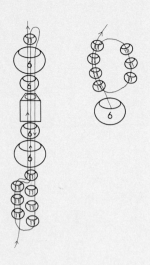

6 Repeat 2; Repeat 3; Repeat 4; Repeat 5; Repeat 2; Repeat 3; Repeat 4; Repeat 5; Repeat 2; Repeat 3; Repeat 4

17 Repeat 5. You should have a rope with 5 lots of A-bead spirals, starting and ending on the A bead spiral.

18 BEAD BREAK Now pick up a 6-mm round bead, 1F 6°, 1 magnetic bead, 1F 6°, a 6-mm round bead, and 1E 11°. Take the thread over the E core bead and back through the 6-mm, F 6°, magnetic bead, F 6°, 6-mm, and up 4E core beads. Turn again towards the head to where you left off, and up the A spiral beside your thread, and once again through the 6-mm, F 6°, magnetic bead, F 6°, 6-mm, and E 11°. You are back to where you left off (Fig A).

19 Pick up 3E 11°, 3A, and push the beads down on the thread. Go back up all 4 core beads (one core bead is already on the rope) (Fig B).

20 Repeat Rows 2 to 19 thirteen times, then repeat Row 2 through to and including Row 17.

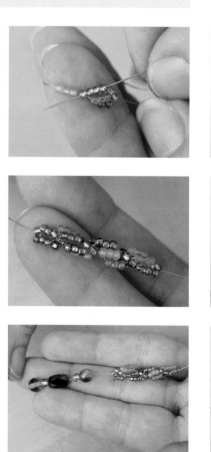

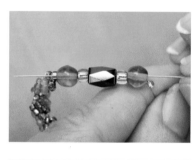

Finishing off

The last piece to the end of your lariat is the bead break. Pick up a 6-mm round bead, 1F 6°, 1 magnetic bead, 1F 6°, and 1E°. Turn. Take the thread over the core bead and back up the F 6°, magnetic bead, F 6° and the 6-mm round bead, and back up 4 core beads. Knot, down the spiral, knot, and back into the bead break, cut. Repeat at the other end.

New thread

If your thread is becoming short, complete a spiral, work up the core, and knot. Leave that thread. It is your maker to where you left off. Take a new thread, travel back through 4 core beads towards the start, and knot into the nearest spiral. Work down that spiral, knot again and work back into the core, travel to where you left off. Continue …

Then pick up the tail, to be fastened properly. Travel up the new core, and knot into the nearest spiral, down that spiral, knot, and back into the core, cut.

It is quite wise to dab a little bit if glue or clear nail varnish very gently on the end knot.

Gail
Spiral rope belt, Method 2

The belt is made using the same method as in the first project – the only difference really being the use of differently sized and shaped beads in slightly varied combinations.

The belt is made up of lots of rope pieces put together, so once you have made the first one, it is just a matter of repetition. The joy of this piece is its versatility – it can be used as a tieback, as a lariat, or wrapped twice around the neck, and so on. I have used 9° and 8° seed beads for the most part, and then magnetic beads, the Indian silver rhombics, and rings. The quantities are for one piece of rope (about 12 cm); the number of these will vary depending on the length of the belt you are making.

You will need
44A 9° Gutermann black
40B 9° Gutermann silver
80C 9° Gutermann gold (core)
25A 8° black seen beads
25B 8° silver seed beads
8D 4-mm Gutermann round beads to match core
4E 8-mm Indian silver rhombic
4F magentic pillars (5x8 mm)
16 to 20-mm jump ring
lobster clasp
16 matching 6-mm round beads for tassel
8 heavy metal beads for tassel
Nymo thread(strong)
#10 beading needle

Thread up with 1,5 m of Nymo thread for each piece of rope. Leave at least 20 cm with which to go back and work later. Now, pick up:

1 4C 9° (these will be the core beads), 3A 9°. Go back up the 4 core beads, from tail to head (Fig A, B).

2 Now pick up 1C 9° plus 1B 9°, 1B 8°, 1B 9°, and back up 3 core and one new one, thus 4C core beads (Fig C, D).

3 Pick up 1C 9° plus 2A 9°, 1A 8°, and back up 3 core and one new one, thus 4 core beads (Fig E).

4 Repeat Rows 2 and 3 five times and you will have 7A spirals in total.

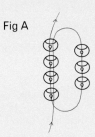

Fig A

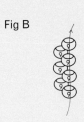

Fig B

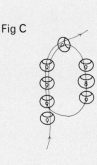

Fig C

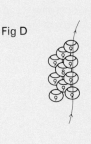

Fig D

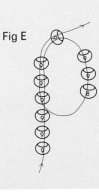

Fig E

14 You will now finish one end. Pick up 1D 4-mm round bead, 1E Indian silver rhombic, 1D 4-mm round bead, 1F magnetic bead, and 7C 9°. Take the thread through the ring, to form a loop over the ring and back down the magnetic bead, D, E, D, and through 4 core beads; snug up. Turn and back to the ring side, down the A spiral, into D, E, D, F, and through the 7 core beads again (the loop). Now into the working part again, through F, D, E, D, and up the A spiral, through 1 core and turn, to the ring side. Now go down the B spiral through 1 core and D, E, D, F, and through the 7 core beads again (you now have 3 threads running through the ring bead loops). Make your way back to where you left off, through the mix of beads up the core and spirals to where the tail thread was left. Knot into the base of the first A spiral. Before bringing your thread out of the core, knot with the old tail, and continue with the working thread.

15 Repeat Rows 2 and 3 (reversing the sequence of Row 3: 1C 9° plus 1 8°, 2A 9°) three times. You now have 10 A spirals in total.

21 Now repeat Row 14, taking the thread back into the main body. Knot twice, and travel. Go back and tidy up the tail end.

Make another rope piece, and attach it into the same ring, side by side. Start the third rope: attach one side to the old ring on the belt, and the other side to a new ring. Continue until you have the desired length. I made 8 segments (16 pieces of rope), starting and ending with a ring.
   Attach a lobster clasp onto one ring, and close.

Tassel

Follow Steps 1, 2, 3, 2, 3, and then 2 again. This is the rope top.
   Now make a tassel from the core using Method 1 (see page 26). Use a heavy bead at the end before turning back up. Now work up the 4 core beads and back down the B spiral, make another tassel. Back up the B spiral and 1 core, and down the next A spiral, and so on
   Make 6 tassels, using the 6-mm round beads as well.
   Make the loop at the top, as you made all the loops over the ring, making a double loop into the one end ring. Now end off.

gail 45

Tina

Spiral rope necklace

This necklace starts off very easy, and progressively gets a little more difficult. Any of the four separate sections can also make up an entire necklace. I love the chips and use them extensively in my work, as they add texture. Try to find the tiny chips for this project. The core down the centre remains the same throughout, but the variation is brought about in the spiral, which I changed on each of the segments, still using only three beads to make up the spiral, and just varying their sizes.

Used three different colours for this design, say black, brown and gold, the gold being the core. The first colour could be brown, so you would need 11°, 8° and 6°seed beads, and small chips in brown. They do not all have to be the same brown, as long as they look good together, for example a lustre 11° seed and a mat 8° seed in medium brown, a clear 6° seed in light brown and a brown chip. Do the same for the black.

Again, it is important to work with a good length of thread – the fewer joins in your work, the better. I find 2,5 m a good length to work with.

For this project you will use a combination of Methods 1 and 2 adding chips. It is a little more challenging as it is not always easy to follow the core.

You will need

10-g A 11° seed beads: core
10-g B 11° seed beads: first colour
10-g C 11° seed beads: second colour
10-g D 8° seed beads: first colour
10-g E 8° seed beads: second colour
10-g F 6° seed beads: first colour
10-g G 6 ° seed beads: second colour
10-g J 6° seed beads: same colour as core
50H small chips stone first colour
50I small chips stone second colour
2 Gutermann 6-mm round beads
4 Gutermann 8-mm round bead
toggle to fasten necklace
6,5 m Nymo D-thread
#11 or 12 beading needle

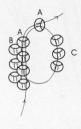

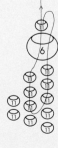

Part 1

Thread up with about 2,5 m of thread, keeping a 20-cm tail.
The first section is worked only in 11° beads.

1 Pick up 4A (these will be the core beads) and 3B and then go through the 4A beads only, again from the tail up. Push the 3B beads to the left (these will form the spiral), leaving the core beads on the right (Fig A, B).

2 Pick up 1A, and 3C, push the beads to the end of the thread, next to your work, and needle up the 3A core beads on the rope and the new core bead you have just added, thus 4A core beads. Push the C spiral to the left so the beads lie on the B spiral. It is important to make sure the spirals are always pushed to the left, and sit neatly on top of each other. Your core will grow one bead at a time (Fig C, D).

3 Pick up 1A and 3B. Push the beads down the thread, and then needle up the 3A core beads on the rope plus the new core bead to make 4A core beads. Push the B spiral to the left to lie on top of the C and B spiral.

4 Repeat steps 2 and 3 twelve times for a longer length (25 spirals, 48 cm). Repeat steps 2 and 3 nine times for a shorter length (21 spirals, 43 cm).

5 Pick up a 6-mm round bead and 1A. Take the needle back over the core bead and through the 6-mm round bead, plus 4A beads, heading towards the beginning, snug up. Turn towards the working end again and down the B spiral, through the 6-mm round bead, and the one core bead. You are back to where you were (Fig E, page 47).

Part 2

You'll now be adding the 8° beads, D and E.

6 Pick up 2A and 3B. Thread back up the 3A core beads on the rope (one core was there, and the two new ones).

7 Pick up 1A, 1C, 1E, 1C. Now thread back up the 3A core beads plus one new core, making 4 core beads.

8 Pick up 1A, 2B, 1D, and back up the 3 core plus the new one, making 4 core beads.

9 Repeat steps 7 and 8 twelve times for the longer length (25 spirals) and ten times for the shorter length (21 spirals).

Part 3

You will now be adding 6° seed beads, F and G.

10 Repeat Step 5 (Part 1), but use an 8-mm round bead.

11 Pick up 2A, 1B, 1D, 1F, and back up the 3 core beads (one was there before, and the two new ones).

12 Pick up 1A, 1G, 1E, 1C, and back up 3 core plus 1 new one, making 4 core beads.

13 Pick up 1A, 1B, 1D, 1F, and back up 3 core plus 1 new one, making 4 core beads.

14 Repeat steps 11 and 12 twelve times to make 25 spirals.

Part 4

You will now be adding the chips, I and J.

15 Repeat Step 5 (Part 1), but use an 8-mm round bead.

16 Pick up 2A, 1B, 1D, 1F. Thread back up the 3 core beads (one core was there before, and the two new ones).

17 Pick up 1A, 1I, 1G, 1E, and go back up 3 core plus 1 new one to make 4 core beads.

18 Pick up 1A, 1D, 1H, 1F, and go back up 3 core plus 1 new one to make 4 core beads.

19 Pick up 1A, 1G, 1E, 1I, and go back up 3 core plus 1 to make 4 core beads.

20 Pick up 1A, 1H, 1A, 1D, and go back up 3 core plus 1 to make 4 core beads.

21 Pick up 1A, 1C, 1I, 1G, and go back up 3 core plus 1 to make 4 core beads.

22 Pick up 1A, 1J, 1H, 1D, and go back up 3 core plus 1 to make 4 core beads.

23 Repeat steps 17 to 22 thirteen times to make 78 spirals

Back to Part 3

Go back to using the 6° bead, only now the parts are in reverse.

24 Repeat Step 5 (Part 1) using an 8-mm round bead.

25 Pick up 2A, 1F, 1D, 1B, and back up 3 core (one was already attached, plus the 2 new core beads.)

26 Pick up 1A, 1C, 1E, 1G, and go back up the 3 core plus the new 1 to make 4 core beads.

27 Pick up 1A, 1F, 1D, 1B, and go back up 3 core plus 1 new to make 4 core beads.

28 Repeat Steps 26 and 27 twelve times to make 25 spirals.

Back to Part 2

Go back to using the 8° seed beads.

29 Repeat Step 5 (Part 1), but use and 8-mm round bead.

30 Pick up 2A, 1D, 2B, and back up the 3 core (one was already attached, plus the 2 new core beads).

31 Pick up 1A, 1C, 1E, 1C, and back up the 3 core plus 1 new one to make 4 core beads.

32 Pick up 1 core bead, 1D, 2B, and back up 3 core plus 1 new one to make 4 core beads.

33 Repeat steps 31 and 32 twelve times for the longer length (25 spirals) and ten times for the shorter length (21 spirals).

Back to Part 1

Now use only the 11° beads.

34 Repeat Step 5 (Part 1) using a 6-mm round bead.

35 Pick up 2A, 3B, and go back up the 3 core beads (one attached plus 2 new core beads).

36 Pick up 1A, 3C, and back up 3 core plus 1 new core bead to make 4 core beads.

37 Pick up 1A, 3B, and back up 3 core plus 1 new core bead to make 4 core beads.

38 Repeat steps 36 and 37 twelve times for the longer length (25 spirals) and ten times for the shorter length (21 spirals).

Your necklace is now complete and only the fastening remains to be finished. I have used a T-bar, which is very easy to do up.

Thread up, or use the working thread, and put on 7A beads, take the needle through the loop on the bar, and back up 4A beads. Turn, and then go down the spiral and through the 7 core beads again. Repeat, so there are 3 threads running through the end beads. Travel and knot, travel and cut. I like to dab a little clear nail varnish where I have ended the thread. Repeat for the other side, using the tail thread that was left. Take the beads through the loop on the ring side and continue to match the first piece.

Brick stitch

Brick stitch is a very useful off-loom stitch that is slightly firmer than peyote stitch. The beads are sewn together in single, double or treble drops, the holes facing north and south. They are sewn very closely together and the stitching forms a fabric that looks just like a brick wall – hence the name of the stitch. Most brick-stitch work is started with a foundation row of ladder stitch. This can be done in two ways, with a single needle or twin needles.

Note that the bookmark on the photograph below is lying on its side. When you work the brick stitch the holes will face north and south.

Ladder stitch

Method 1 (using a single needle)

Pick up two beads A, B, and needle back through the first bead A. Holding the two beads between the thumb and first finger, the thread comes out of the top of the back bead; take the needle down through the B bead, bringing the thread to the front bead.

Pick up a new bead, C, and take the needle back through the top of the B bead to attach it, and finish the stitch by taking the needle up through the C bead, again bringing the thread to the newest bead.

Pick up a new bead, D, attach it to the C bead by taking the needle up the C bead, and then back down the D bead. Continue as from the C bead.

You will see that one bead is attached in a clockwise direction, and then the next in an anticlockwise direction. Having finished the ladder stitch, you can stabilise the row by going back in and out. Do make sure you do not twist the beads. If you are going to join the beads, just continue, but instead of picking up a bead, use the first bead of the row, where you started.

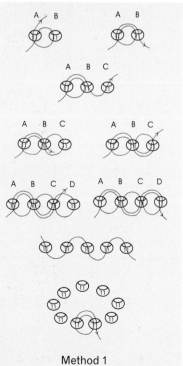

Method 1

Method 2 (using two needles)

With this method two needles are used. The work is not as strong as the first, as it has less thread going through. Some people find that it is easier to obtain the right amount of tension using this method.

Thread up with a good long thread (about 2,5 m), a needle on both sides.

Pick up a bead, and centre the bead on the thread.

Pick up another bead with the left needle, and push it down the thread on top of the first bead. Holding the beads between your thumb and first finger, bring the thread to the right. Now take the right needle through the same bead, entering the bead where your thread came out. Snug up, pull both right and left needles.

The threads cross in the centre of the bead.

To join together, go through the first bead of the row, in the same manner with your left and right needles. Then continue through at least 5 more, to stop it slipping. Unthread one needle (you will come back to that thread at a later stage), and continue with the threaded needle.

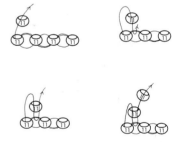

Method 2

Flat brick-stitch

Brick stitch can be worked from left to right or right to left. I prefer working from left to right, which means I turn my work, making the reading of a graph a little harder. I also like to work flat brick with short rows and long rows alternating, as I find it gives me a good, firm edge.

Your thread has come out of the end bead in the foundation row. Pick up a bead.

Pick up the thread between the beads of the row below. Now back up through the bead you have just picked up.

Pick up another bead, and continue in the same fashion until the end of the row. Work the last bead into the last thread between the beads. This is a short row, because there is one fewer bead.

To make a long row, you will increase at the beginning of the row, by one bead, and again at the end of the row, by one bead.

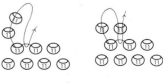

Flat brick-stitch

Increase at the beginning of the row with one bead

Pick up 2 beads and work into the first pocket (the thread between the beads) of the row below (Fig A, B).

Fig A   Fig B

Increase at the beginning

Increase at the end

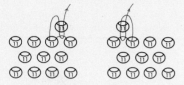

Concealed thread

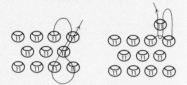

Start of row

Decrease

Decrease in the centre

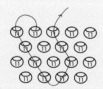

Decrease more than one at start

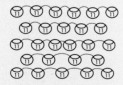

Increase in the middle

Increase at end of the row with one bead

Having worked the last bead in the last pocket, pick up a new bead and take the needle through the last bead in the row below, and the second last bead in the 2nd row below the worked row. Make a figure 8 entering in the last bead of the same row, and coming out of the second bead on the working row.

Concealed thread

Start of a new short row.

I like to conceal the outer thread, so having come out of the second bead, I now work one bead to the right of my thread, then turn my work and continue. Alternatively you could come out of the end bead, but this way the thread will be visible.

Decrease

Work only short rows, and you will have a natural decrease.

Decrease in the centre of the row

To decrease in the centre of your work, miss one pocket between the beads, and work the rest of the row as usual. Next row work as usual.

Decrease more than 1 bead at the start of the row

Having put in the last bead of the row, you need to decrease by two or three beads. Travel down two rows, and come up where you need to.

In this case I have come out in the 3rd bead and have decreased by 2 beads, or by one bead if using the concealed method.

To increase in the middle of a row

Work a row normally until you get to where you would like to increase. Work two beads into one pocket. The next row you will work normally, one bead in each pocket.

Reading a graph (pattern)

If you're working flat brick stitch, you will read the pattern from the sides for the short rows, and from left to right for the long rows. I like to make a little mark as my work grows to keep my place.

If you're working tubular brick stitch the graph is read going round and round. As you step up for each row, the starting point moves over by one bead, so very often this is marked with a line through the pattern. Some of the beads are marked.

Reading a graph

Tubular brick stitch

Having worked the foundation row with ladder stitch, and joined it as above, you will now start the tubular brick stitch. To start the row:

Pick up 2 beads and work the second bead into the second pocket , leaving the first bead loose, wobbling slightly angled on the thread before the second bead.

Continue to work brick as normal, until you come to the end of the row.

Work the last bead in the last pocket, and then join up with the first wobbly bead. Take your needle down the wobbly bead and brick into it in the same manner as you have used with all the beads. This will pull the wobbly bead straight, and give you a tidy end.

Now you will start the new row. Your thread will be coming out of the first bead in the last row, thus your starting point has moved over by one bead (see *Reading a graph*, above). To start the new row, pick up 2 beads as before and work as before.

Tubular brick-stitch

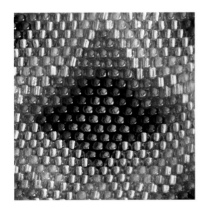

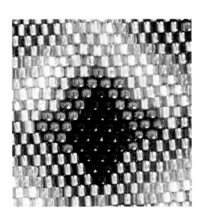

Aide
Bookmark, using flat brick-stitch

This bookmark is the perfect little gift for a bookworm. Using different colours you can make many bookmarks and make each look quite unique and different.

It is important to use a good quality bead, as the regularity of the beads is going to make all the difference to your work. I have used Japanese beads, because they have larger holes. I have used 11° beads, which gives a lovely fabric. In addition I used the concealed side-thread method, made up with short and long rows, using four colours. I find it a good policy to use a ballpoint beading needle when making straight brick. You do not need the point of the needle, and there will be less chance of you accidentally splitting the thread. You could also easily turn the bookmark into a choker or bracelet by simply adding a button to one end and a loop to the other.

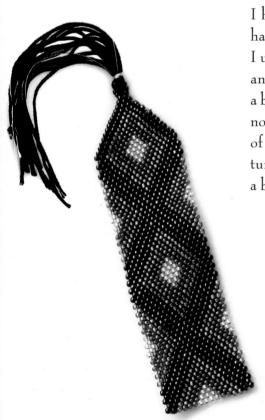

You will need
290A 11° dark
210B 11° medium
130C 11° medium light
50D 11° light
10 m Nymo thread
11 or 12 beading needle
2 m perlé no 8 or no 5 for tassel
metallic thread (optional)

Thread up with a good long thread, about 2,5 m. Use the foundation or ladder-stitch method and leave a tail of about 1 m in length. You will come back to use this thread.

1 Foundation row: pick up 2A, 2B, 2C, 4D, 2C, 2B, 2A (16 beads).

Start the brick work

Start Row 2 with brick stitch (Fig A).

Having put on the last bead on a long row, come out the second bead in from the end, and work one bead on the end. Then turn your work once your thread is out of the bead on the new row, and work back as usual (Fig B, C).

In Row 3, increase by 1 (see page 53 Fig A, B).

In Row 4, use the concealed thread method (Fig C).

foundation

foundation

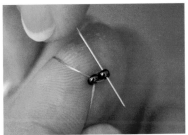

foundation

foundation

foundation

foundation

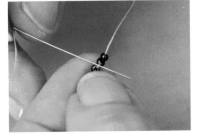

start brick

start brick

Foundation or
Ladder stitch (method 1)

Fig A: Start the brick work

Fig B: Start new row

Fig C: Turn and continue

Fig D: Fix the last bead

ROW	PICK-UP	RESULT
2	2A, 2B, 2C, 3D, 2C, 2B, 2A	15 beads, short row
3	3A, 2B, 2C, 2D, 2C, 2B, 3A	16 beads, long row
4	3A, 2B, 2C, 1D, 2C, 2B, 3A	15 beads, short row
5	4A, 2B, 4C, 2B, 4A	16 beads, long row
6	4A, 2B, 3C, 2B, 4A	15 beads, short row
7	1B, 4A, 2B, 2C, 2B, 4A, 1B	16 beads, long row
8	1B, 4A, 2B, 1C, 2B, 4A, 1B	15 beads, short row
9	2B, 4A, 4B, 4A, 2B	16 beads, long row
10	2B, 4A, 3B, 4A, 2B	15 beads, short row
11	1C, 2B, 4A, 2B, 4A, 2B, 1C	16 beads, long row
12	1C, 2B, 4A, 1B, 4A, 2B, 1C	15 beads, short row
13	2C, 2B, 8A, 2B, 2C	16 beads, long row
14	2C, 2B, 7A, 2B, 2C	15 beads, short row
15	1D, 2C, 2B, 6A, 2B, 2C, 1D	16 beads, long row
16	1D, 2C, 2B, 5A, 2B, 2C, 1D	15 beads, short row
17	2D, 2C, 2B, 4A, 2B, 2C, 2D	16 beads, long row
18	1D, 2C, 2B, 5A, 2B, 2C, 1D	15 beads, short row
19	1D, 2C, 2B, 6A, 2B, 2C, 1D	16 beads, long row
20	repeat 14	15 beads, short row
21	repeat 13	16 beads, long row
22	repeat 12	15 beads, short row

ROW	PICK-UP	RESULT
23	repeat 11	16 beads, long row
24	repeat 10	15 beads, short row
25	repeat 9	16 beads, long row
26	repeat 8	15 beads, short row
27	repeat 7	16 beads, long row
28	repeat 6	15 beads, short row
29	repeat 5	16 beads, long row
30	repeat 4	15 beads, short row
31	repeat 3	16 beads, long row
32	repeat 2	15 beads, short row
33	2A, 2B, 2C, 4D, 2C, 2B, 2A	16 beads, long row

Fig A: Long row / short row

1– 33 = 1 pattern. Now repeat once more, from row 2 = 65 rows.

Now, start to decrease on both sides to bring it to a closure. If you work short rows each time, you will have a natural decrease. After each row, turn and then start to brick in the first pocket (Fig B).

Fig B: Natural decrease

66	2A, 2B, 2C, 3D, 2C, 2B, 2A	15 beads
67	2A, 2B, 2C, 2D, 2C, 2B, 2A	14 beads
68	2A, 2B, 2C, 1D, 2C, 2B, 2A	13 beads
69	2A, 2B, 4C, 2B, 2A	12 beads
70	2A, 2B, 3C, 2B, 2A	11 beads
71	2A, 2B, 2C, 2B, 2A	10 beads
72	2A, 2B, 1C, 2B, 2A	9 beads
73	2A, 4B, 2A	8 beads
74	2A, 3B, 2A	7 beads
75	2A, 2B, 2A	6 beads
76	2A, 1B, 2A	5 beads
77	4A	4 beads
78	3A	3 beads
79	2A	11 beads

You have completed the end of the bookmark with brick.

Your thread comes out of one of the top beads. Pick up 7A and take your needle down the other top bead; you have formed a loop.

Travel a little and repeat the last action, out of the top bead, and through the loop and back into the body. I like to always put 3 threads through my loops to strengthen them.

Bracelet

If you wish to make a bracelet, then the other side also needs to be tapered. Repeat from Row 66. Maak a loop and an end button, or attach any other Fastener.

Tassel

Cut about 6 pieces of perlé no 8 or 5 about 30 cm long, and thread them through the loop. I also put in a little metallic thread. Fold in half, and then bind. I wrapped a little metallic thread carefully and neatly next to each other to bind it, finished it off with a button-hole stitch, and took my thread to the inside. Once the threads are secure, cut your tassel neatly.

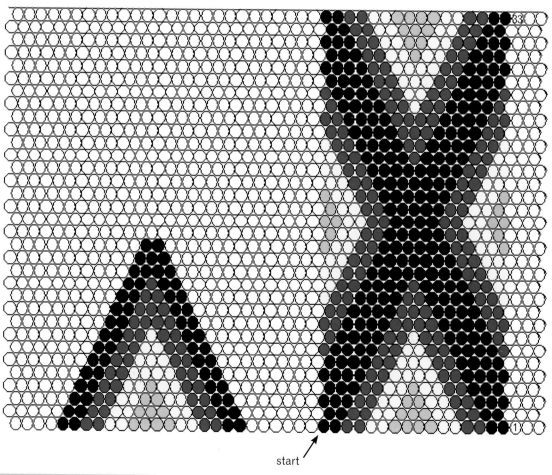

start

Tosca
Tubular brick amulet

The amulet bag dates back many centuries and was first made of animal skin or cloth. Today we can happily make them with beads, to be worn around the neck or as a little pouch in which to keep a lucky charm or a birthstone.

I very often use an amulet bag to introduce a new beader to small beads. There is something extremely satisfying about making the fabric and watching the pattern grow. I have again used Japanese seed beads 11°. As for the previous project, when making a type of bead fabric, the regularity and the uniformity of the beads are going to make the world of difference to the outcome of your project.

The ladder stitch, or foundation row, is joined together to make a tube. I used the Method 2, which requires the use of two needles. Each brick row is finished, and then the new row is started. If you spiral, you have not joined a row properly.

I prefer using a ballpoint needle, as I don't like splitting the thread. Use a short needle to weave the body, and a long needle for the tassels.

You will need

600A 11° seed beads, silver (background)

250B 11° seed beads, light blue

240C 11° seed beads, turquoise (light medium)

255D 11° seed beads, emerald (medium)

240E 11° seed beads, dark blue

60F 11° seed beads, lime (contrast)

For the tassel and strap

Seed beads as above, plus

130A, 30E 8° (silver, dark blue)

30 each A, C, D, E 6° (silver, turquoise, emerald, dark blue)

30A 7-mm Gutermann bugles

10A 4-mm Gutermann round beads

30A and 5 each C, D, E, F 6-mm Gutermann round beads

5 each A, E 8-mm Gutermann round beads

8A and B assorted large shaped beads

15A 4-mm square beads

Nymo thread to match A

#11 or 12 beading needles, short and long

Fig A   Fig B

Fig C

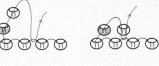

Fig D   Fig E

Fig F

Fig G

Thread up with a long thread: 3 m is quite manageable, as you will leave half behind after the foundation row to use at a later stage. You start at the top of the amulet, so use the two-needle method as the thread is less visible. Put on 44A 11° (Fig A, B).

To close the foundation row, continue working the ladder stitch through another 5 beads to make sure it does not slip. Do be careful when joining not to twist the beads. Make sure all the holes lie the same way, or the brick stitching will not meet (Fig C).

Unthread one needle and leave that thread. Start working with the other needle. I prefer working from left to right. Start your pattern at the beginning of each row and pick up two beads to start with. Miss the first pocket and work into the second (Fig D, E).

STEP	PICK UP
1	1A, 1B, into the second pocket, 2A, 2B, 2C, 2D, 2E, 1F, 2E, 2D, 2C, 2B, 2A, 1B, 2A, 2B, 2C, 2D, 2E, 1F, 2E, 2D, 2C, 2B, 1A and join

You will start a new row out of the first bead of the last row, so the starting bead moves over by one bead each time. Your thread will be out of the wobbly bead (Fig F, G page 63).

2	2B, into the second pocket, 3A, 1C, 3D, 2E, 2F, 2E, 3D, 1C, 3A, 2B, 3A, 1C, 3D, 2E, 2F, 2E, 3D, 1C, 3A and join
3	1C, 1B, into the second pocket, 3A, 2D, 3E, 3F, 3E, 2D, 3A, 1B, 1C, 1B, 3A, 2D, 3E, 3F, 3E, 2D, 3A, 1B and join
4	1C, 1B, into the second pocket, 4A, 3E, 4F, 3E, 4A, 1B, 2C, 1B, 4A, 3E, 4F, 3E, 4A, 1B, 1C and join
5	1C, 1B, into the second pocket, 4A, 2E, 5F, 2E, 4A, 1B, 1C, 1D, 1C, 1B, 4A, 2E, 5F, 2E, 4A,1B, 1C, 1D and join
6	1C, 1B, into the second pocket, 5A, 1E, 4F, 1E, 5A, 1B, 1C, 2D, 1C, 1B, 5A, 1E, 4F, 1E, 5A, 1B, 1C, 2D and join
7	1C, 1B, into the second pocket, 1B, 5A, 3F, 5A, 2B, 1C, 3D, 1C, 2B, 5A, 3F, 5A, 2B, 1C, 3D and join
8	2C, into second pocket, 2B, 4A, 2F, 4A, 2B, 2C, 4D, 2C, 2B, 4A, 2F, 4A, 2B, 2C, 4D and join
9	2C, into second pocket, 2B, 4A, 1F, 4A, 2B, 2C, 2D, 1E, 2D, 2C, 2B, 4A, 1F, 4A, 2B, 2C, 2D, 1E, 2D and join
10	1D, 1C, into the second pocket, 1C, 2B, 6A, 2B, 2C, 2D, 4E, 2D, 2C, 2B, 6A, 2B, 2C, 2D, 4E, 1D and join

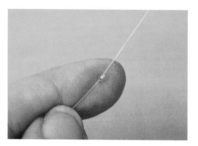
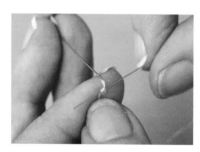
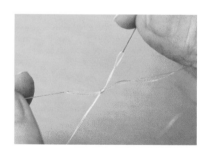

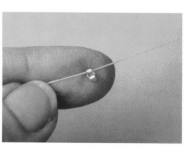
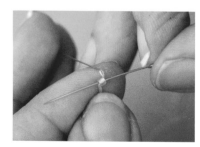
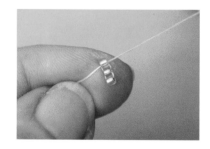

STEP	PICK UP
11	1D, 1C, into the second pocket, 1C, 2B, 2A, 1B, 2A, 2B, 2C, 2D, 2E, 1F, 2E, 2D, 2C, 2B, 2A, 1B, 2A, 2B, 2C, 2D, 2E, 1F, 2E, 1D and join
12	2D, and into the second pocket, 1C, 3A, 2B, 3A, 1C, 3D, 2E, 2F, 2E, 3D, 1C, 3A, 2B, 3A, 1C, 3D, 2E, 2F, 2E, 1D and join
13	2D, and into the second pocket, 3A, 1B, 1C, 1B, 3A, 2D, 3E, 3F, 3E, 2D, 3A, 1B, 1C, 1B, 3A, 2D, 3E, 3F, 3E and join
!4	1D, 1A, and into second pocket, 2A, 1B, 2C, 1B, 3A, 1D, 3E, 4F, 3E, 1D, 3A, 1B, 2C, 1B, 3A, 1D, 3E, 4F, 3E and join
15	2A, and into the second pocket, 1A, 1B, 1C, 1D, 1C, 1B, 4A, 2E, 5F, 2E, 4A, 1B, 1C, 1D, 1C, 1B, 4A, 2E, 5F, 2E, 1A and join
16	2A, and into the second pocket, 1B, 1C, 2D, 1C, 1B, 5A, 1E, 4F, 1E, 5A, 1B, 1C, 2D, 1C, 1B, 5A, 1E, 4F, 1E, 3A and join
17	2B, and into the second pocket, 1C, 3D, 1C, 2B, 5A, 3F, 5A, 2B, 1C, 3D, 1C, 2B, 5A, 3F, 5A and join
18	2C, and into the second pocket, 4D, 2C, 2B, 4A, 2F, 4A, 2B, 2C, 4D, 2C, 2B, 4A, 2F, 4A, 2B and join
19	1C, 1D, and into the second pocket, 1D, 1E, 2D, 2C, 2B, 4A, 1F 4A, 2B, 2C, 2D, 1E, 2D, 2C, 2B, 4A, 1F, 4A, 2B, 1C and join
20	1D, 1E, and into the second pocket, 3E, 2D, 2C, 2B, 6A, 2B, 2C, 2D, 4E, 2D, 2C, 2B, 6A, 2B, 2C, 1D and join
21	2E, and into the second pocket, 1F 2E, 2D, 2C, 2B, 2A, 1B, 2A, 2B, 2C, 2D, 2E, 1F, 2E, 2D, 2C, 2B, 2A, 1B, 2A, 2B, 2C, 2D and join

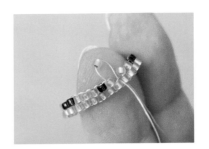

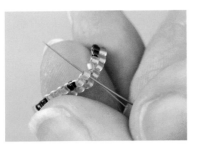

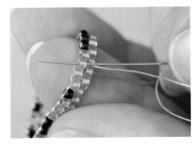

If you've made a mistake and have to undo your work at all, it is easier to unthread the needle and pull out each bead, as you don't want to split the thread.

STEP	PICK UP
22	1E, 1F, and into the second pocket, 1F, 2E, 2D, 2C, 3A, 2B, 3A, 2C, 2D, 2E, 2F, 2E, 2D, 2C, 3A, 2B, 3A, 2C, 2D, 1E and join
23	2F, and into the second pocket, 1F, 3E, 2D, 3A, 1B, 1C, 1B, 3A, 2D, 3E, 3F, 3E, 2D, 3A, 1B, 1C, 1B, 3A, 2D, 3E and join
24	2F, and into the second pocket, 1F, 3E, 1D, 3A, 1B, 2C, 1B, 3A, 1D, 3E, 4F, 3E, 1D, 3A, 1B, 2C, 1B, 3A, 1D, 3E, 1F and join
25	2F, and into the second pocket, 1F, 2E, 4A, 1B, 1C, 1D, 1C, 1B, 4A, 2E, 5F, 2E, 4A, 1B, 1C, 1D, 1C, 1B, 4A, 2E, 2F and join
26	2F, and into the second pocket, 1E, 5A, 1B, 1C, 2D, 1C, 1B, 5A, 1E, 4F, 1E, 5A, 1B 1C, 2D, 1C, 1B, 5A, 1E, 2F and join
27	1F, 1A, and into the second pocket, 4A, 2B, 1C, 3D, 1C, 2B, 5A, 3F, 5A, 2B, 1C, 3D, 1C, 2B, 5A, 2F and join
28	2A, and into the second pocket, 2A, 2B, 2C, 4D, 2C, 2B, 4A, 2F, 4A, 2B, 2C, 4D, 2C, 2B, 4A, 2F and join

STEP	PICK UP
29	2A, and into the second pocket, 1A, 2B, 2C, 2D, 1E, 2D, 2C, 2B, 4A, 1F, 4A, 2B, 2C, 2D, 1E, 2D, 2C, 2B, 4A, 1F, 1A and join
30	1A, 1B, and into the second pocket, 1B, 2C, 2D, 4E, 2D, 2C, 2B, 6A, 2B, 2C, 2D, 4E, 2D, 2C, 2B, 5A and join
31	2B, and into the second pocket, 2C, 2D, 2E, 1F, 2E, 2D, 2C, 2B, 2A, 1B, 2A, 2B, 2C, 2D, 2E, 1F, 2E, 2D, 2C, 2B, 2A, 1B, 2A

Fig A

New thread

Never let your thread become too short. You should always have enough thread on your needle to travel. Having finished the thread, complete the brick stitch and unthread your needle. You will have thread left over from the foundation row – use this first. Make sure that you finish the row near the old thread, and then weave the new thread to the same place you left off and continue (Fig A). Thread up with the old thread, and weave it in the new work (Fig B). Proceed with the brick stitch. Once you have covered the place you left off with the new brick, tidy away the old thread by taking it up into the new work.

Fig B

Sewing up

Fold the bag in half, using the single B bead as your halfway marker. One B will fall to the front on the side, and the other will fall to the back, on the side (Fig C). You should have a partner for each bead opposite it (not of the same colour). Now bring your thread out of the B bead at the base and take the thread under the thread next to it, and the same on the other side, then over the same two threads and under the first one (Fig D, E).

Now bring it across and under the second bead, then over the top and under the two threads of the second two beads (Fig F).

All the slanted stitches go under the threads, and all the top threads are straight. Do not pull on them too forcefully. Each bead should have a partner bead opposite. From these your tassels will be made.

Fig C

Fig D

Fig E

Fig F

New thread

Amulet tassels

The tassels lie on either side of the bag. You will come out one side of the bag, pick up the beads, and go back in on the other side – the tassels straddling the bag (Fig G). I have made the tassels using beads of various sizes, because I like the texture. But there is nothing preventing you from using beads of the same size, if you prefer.

Put in a new 2-m thread. Make sure it is fastened properly, and come out of the A bead on the end, needle facing down, and ready to put on the first tassel.

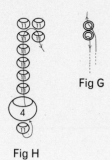

Fig G

Fig H

Amulet tassels

Tassel 1 3A, 2B, 2C, 2D, 3E, 2F all 11°, 1A 4-mm round, 1A 11°, and turn over the 11° seed and take the needle into the 4-mm round and back through all the other beads to the top. Then enter the amulet, needle up through the B bead on the other side (front), which is the partner bead. Then turn and needle down through the adjacent A bead on the same side of the amulet body, ready for tassel 2 (Fig G, H and see Method 1, page 26).

Tassel 2 4A, 1B, 1C, 2D, 2E, 3F, all 11°, 1A 8°, 1A 11°, 1A 4-mm round, 1A 11°. Turn up through all the beads, and enter the A bead in the body of the amulet, on the back side. Turn again and needle down the adjacent B bead, ready for tassel 3. You will make this turn for each tassel (Fig H).

Tassel 3 6A, 1B, 1C, 2D, 1A, all 11°, 1A 8°, 1 bugle, 1A 8°, 1A 11°, 1A 4-mm round, 1A 11°. Turn up into the bag, and back round out of the next bead (B), ready for tassel 4.

Tassel 4 8A, 1B. 1C, 2A, all 11°, 1A 8°, 1 bugle, 1A 8°, 1A 6°, 1 A 6-mm round, 1A 11°. Turn back up and into the bag. Turn for tassel 5.

Tassel 5 1C, 8A, 1B, 2A, all 11°, 1A 8°, 1 bugle, 1A 8°, 1A 11°, 1A 6°, 1A 6-mm round, 1A 11°. Turn back up into the bag, and turn for tassel 6.

Tassel 6 2 C, 1D, 4A, all 11°, 1A 8°, 4A 11°, 2A 8°, 1 bugle, 2B 11°, 1A 8°, 1A 6°, 1A square 4-mm, 1A 6-mm round, and 1A 11°, and turn.

Tassel 7 4D, 2A, all 11°, 1A 8°, 3A 11°, 3A 8°, 1 bugle, 1B 11°, 1C 11°, 1C 6°, 1A 8°, 1A 6°, 1A square 4-mm, 1A 6-mm round , 1A 11°, and then turn.

Tassel 8 2D, 4E, 4A, all 11°, 1A 8°, 3A 11°, 3A 8°, 1 bugle, 1B 11°, 1C 11°, 1C 6°, 1D 6°, 1A 8°, 1A 6°, 1 square 4-mm, 1A 6-mm round, 1A 11°, and turn.

Tassel 9 4E, 1F, 2E, 4A, all 11°, 7A 8°, 1 bugle, 1B 11°, 1C 11°, 1C 6°, 1D 6°, 1A 8°, 1A 6°, 1 square 4-mm, 1A 8°, 1A 6-mm round , 1A 11°, and turn.

Tassel 10 3E, 5F, 3A, all 11°seed, 7A 8°, 1 bugle, 1B 11°, 1C 11°, 1C 6°, 1D 6°, 1E 6°, 1A 6°, 1 square 4-mm, 1A 8°, 1A 6-mm round, 1A 11°, and turn.

Tassel 11 11F 11°, 8A 8°, 1 bugle, 1B 11°, 1C11°, 1C 6°, 1D 6°, 1E 6°, 1A 6°, 1 square 4-mm, 1A 8°, 1A 6-mm round, 1A 11°, and turn.

This is halfway in the tassel, the other side is a repeat of this

12 Repeat 11, repeat 10, repeat 9, and so on to the end of the bag.

Having put the last tassel in, weave the thread up and down to make sure it is very well secured, before cutting.

Amulet beaded rope

You're now ready to put on the rope. String one rope of beads, using all the mixed beads, small and large. Then go back and strengthen the smaller beads with a second string.

Fold the bag as you did for the base, with the B bead on either side, one on the front, and one on the back under the A row.

There are 6 larger beads in the string. Choose any colour you like, just remember to match the second side to the first.

Thread up with 3 times the length of the rope (for example, if your rope is 68 cm, use 204 cm of thread). Fasten well into the bag, coming out of the A bead on one side (Fig A). Now pick up:

1 3C 11°, 1B 11°, 1A 11°, 1 bugle, 2C 11°, 1E 6°, 1E 8-mm round, 1E 6°, 5A 11°, 1A 6°, 3E 11°, 1A 4-mm round, 3E 11°, 2A 8°, and one larger shaped bead.

2 1A 6-mm round, 3B 11°, 2E 11°, 6D 11°, 1D 6°, 1D 6-mm round, 1D 6°, 2D 11°, 3E 11°, 1E 6°, 1F 6-mm round, and one larger shaped bead.

3 1A 6-mm round, 1C 6°, 3C 11°, 4B 11°, 4A 8°, 1 bugle, 3A 8°, 1A 8-mm round, 3A 8°, 1A 4-mm round, 3D 11°, 5E 11°, 1 E 6-mm round, 1E 8-mm round, 1E 6°, 5A 8°, 1A 6-mm round, 3E 11°, 1A 4-mm round, 3E 11°, 2A 8°, and one larger shaped bead.

4 1A 6-mm round, 3B 11°, 6D 11°, 1D 6°, 1D 6-mm round, 1D 6°, 2D 11°, 3E 11°, 1E 6°, 1F 6-mm round, 1A 8°, 1 bugle, 1A 8°, 1A 8-mm round. This is halfway on the rope.

Now continue with the other side matching the first half while working backwards. For example, continue with: 1A 8°, 1 bugle, 1A 8°, 1F 6-mm round, 1E 6°, and so on.

Having completed the rope, join it to the other side of the bag – on the same side as the strap, either on the back or the front. You will use the other side bead on the front or the back (the partner bead) to strengthen the handle (Fig B).

Now fasten the thread by travelling up and down the brick work in the bag. Come out of the other side bead of the front or back (partner bead), ready to strengthen the handle. Using the same thread, pick up:

Fig A

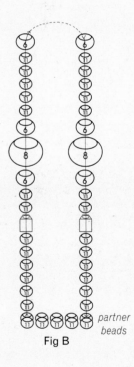

partner beads

Fig B

Amulet beaded rope

Fig C

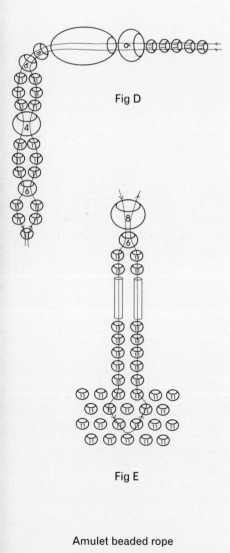

Fig D

Fig E

Amulet beaded rope

5 3C 11°, 1B 11°, 1A 11°, 1 bugle, 2C 11°, and up through the E 6°, and 1E 8-mm round, and 1E 6° that is on the rope already (Fig E). Then pick up 2A 11° and miss 2A 11° on the existing rope, and through the next A 11°. Pick up another 2A 11° and through the large A 6° on the rope (Fig C).

6 Now pick up 3E 11°, and through the 1A 4-mm round, pick up another 3E 11° and then take your thread through all the beads on the rope until you get to the other side, by the bag where you have the large shaped bead (Fig D). Strengthen as you did the first side, in other words, out of the large A 6°, pick up 3E 11° and through the A 4-mm round – continue.

7 Having put on the last 3C 11°, fasten into the partner bead in the front or back, weaving the thread away.

Take a new thread 3 times the length of the rope. Put a needle on either side of the thread and weave the thread into the bag – one needle coming out of the handle on the front, and the other coming out of the handle on the back. Go through all the beads again using the twin needles to travel up the handles together on either side, coming together in the single rope. You should have 4 threads going through the rope.

Fasten off by weaving the thread os one needle into the front of the bag and the other into the back of the bag.

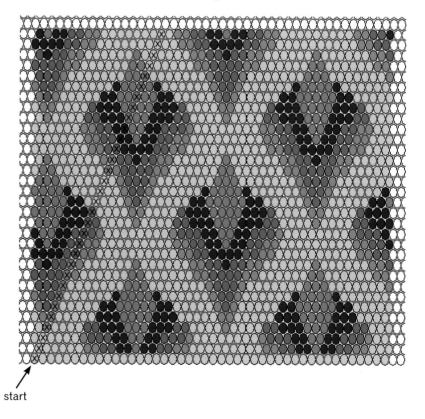

start

Anna

Brick necklace, using flat brick-stitch with decrease within the row

I have used a variety of different beads to make this necklace, some to add interest and others to give texture. The necklace has a slightly Victorian feel, yet can be very modern. It looks lovely in a single colour, broken up by many colours or in two tones as I have done here. Have fun playing with it. By decreasing and using beads of different sizes, you will be able to get a good curve for the neck – and then the variation is endless. I have used Method 1 to make the foundation row, but Method 2 will work just as well. Do make sure you start with a long thread, because the last thing you want to do is have to change thread in the first row. This necklace measures 39 cm.

You will need
8-g A 11° main colour
8-g B 11° contrast
12-g A 8° main colour
4-g A 6° main colour
30B 14° for clasp
14B 7-mm bugle contrast
16C 3-mm squares to tone with A
6A 4-mm squares main colour
20D 4-mm squares to tone with B
18A 4-mm faceted main colour
18B 4-mm faceted contrast
10 m Nymo D-thread
#11 or 12 beading needle

Because bead sizes do vary a little it may be necessary to add an extra bead to the tassels now and then.

Fig A

Fig B

Fig C

Fig D

Fig E

Fig G

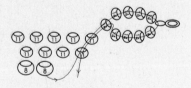
Fig H

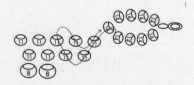
Fig I

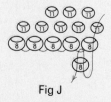
Fig J

1 Thread up with 2,5 m of Nymo D. Start with the foundation row, as in method, 1 as it is very strong. Start with the narrowest part of the necklace and the smallest bead. Using ladder stitch put on between 180 and 200 beads in A11° (this necklace is 39 cm and I used 180 beads). Add the beads in multiples of 4, for example 180, or 184, 188, and so on (Fig, A, B, C).

2 Brick another row. This will be a short row, so start in the first pocket with A11° (Fig D, E).

3 Now change to seed A8° and miss the first pocket and then brick 2A and miss a pocket, and brick 3A miss a pocket and brick another 3A, continue miss a pocket, and brick 3, all the way to the end. The last will be to brick 2 and miss the last pocket, as you are decreasing the number of beads you are using (Fig G).

4 Time to add the clasp. Take the needle diagonally up to the first row, out of the top bead. Pick up 5B 14°, then the clasp, then another 4B 14°, and take the needle through the first 14°, making a loop. Now work down the A bead you came out of and the bead below it (the two end beads). Now work diagonally up bead 2 on row 2 and bead 3 on the first row, down bead 2, and back up the first bead to repeat the loop. Repeat again so there are 3 threads running through (Fig H, I).

5 Make your way out of the bead at the bottom to continue a straight row of brick with A 8°, starting in the first pocket (Fig J).

6 Mark the centre of the row. I put a needle up the centre bead and count 15 beads on either side of the centre bead. Mark as well. These will be for the 31 tassels. Make the edging up to the first marked point (Fig K).

Make the edging brick again but pick up 2 beads at a time. Your thread is out of the large bead on the end. Now pick up 2A 11° and brick into the first pocket, taking the needle back through the last bead only. From then on pick up 1B and 1A, and brick into the next pocket, taking the needle back through only the A bead (Fig L, M).

With the last edge bead, pick up two beads, and instead of working into the pocket, take the needle up the first tassel bead, then circle stitch (Fig N). Come out of the same bead, ready for your first tassel.

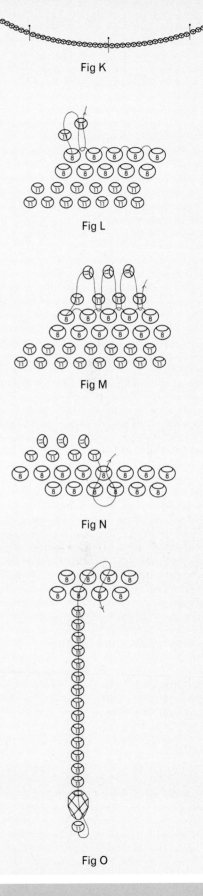

Fig K

Fig L

Fig M

Fig N

Fig O

TASSEL	PICK UP
1	14A 11°, 1A 4-mm facetted, 1B 11° and turn (Fig O)
2	13A 11°, 1A 8°, 2A 11°,1 B 4-mm faceted, 1B 11° and turn
3	11A 11°, 1A 8°, 1B bugle, 1A 8°, 1A 11°, 1A 4-mm facetted, 1B 11° and turn
4	12A 11°, 1A 8°,1B bugle, 1A 8°, 1A 6°, 1B 4-mm facetted, 1B 11°, and turn
5	13A 11°, 1A 8°, 1B bugle , 1A 11°, 1A 8°, 1A 6°, 1A 4-mm facetted, 1B 11°, and turn
6	7A 11°, 1A 8°, 4A 11°, 2A 8°, 1B bugle, 2A 11°, 1A 8°, 1A 6°, 1B 4-mm facetted, 1B 11°, and turn
7	8A 11°, 1A 8°, 4A 11°, 2A 8°, 1B bugle, 2A 11°, 1A 6°, 1A 8°, 1B 4-mm square, 1A 4-mm facetted, 1B 11°, and turn
8	4A 11°, 1A 8°, 3A 11°, 1A 8°, 3A 11°, 3A 8°, 1B bugle, 2A 11°, 1A 8°, 1A 6° 1A 8°, 1C 3-mm square, 1B 4-mm facetted, 1B 11°, and turn
9	1A 8°, 3A 11°, 1A 8°, 3A 11°, 1A 8°, 2A 11°, 4A 8°, 1B bugle, 2A 11°, 1A 8°, 1A 6°, 1A 8°, 1A 6° 1B 4-mm square, 1A 4-mm facetted, 1B 11°, and turn
10	1A 8°, 3A 11°, 1A 8°, 3A 11°, 1A 8°, 2A 11°, 5A 8°, 1B bugle, 1A 11°, 1C 3-mm square, 1A 8° 1A 6°, 1 8°, 1A 6°, 1B 4-mm facetted, 1B 11°, and turn
11	1A 8°, 3A 11°, 1A 8°, 3A 11°, 2A 8°, 2A 11°, 6A 8°, 1B bugle, 1A 11°, 1 C 3-mm square, 1A 8°, 1A 6°, 1A 8°, 1B 4-mm square, 1A 4-mm facetted, 1B 11°, and turn
12	2A 8°, 3A 11°, 1A 8°, 2A 11, 2A 8°, 2A 11°, 7A 8°, 1B bugle, 1A 11°, 1C 3-mm square, 4A 6°, 1B 4-mm facetted, 1A 11°, and turn
13	2A 8°, 3A 11°, 1A 8°, 2A 11, 2A 8°, 2A 11°, 8A 8°, 1B bugle, 1A 11°, 1C 3-mm square, 1A 6°, 1A 4-mm square, 1A 8°, 1B 4-mm square, 1A 4-mm facetted, 1B 11°, and turn
14	2A 8°, 3A 11°, 1A 8°, 2A 11°, 2A 8°, 1A 11°, 9A 8°, 1B bugle, 1A 11°, 1C 3-mm square, 2A 8°, 3A 6°, 1B 4-mm facetted, 1B 11°, and turn
15	3A 8°, 3A 11°, 3A 8°, 1A 11°, 3A 8°, 1C 3-mm square, 3A 8°, 1C 3-mm square, 1A 8°, 1B bugle, 1A 11°, 1C 3-mm square, 1A 6°, 1A 4-mm square, 1A 8°, 1A 6°, 1B 4-mm square, 1A 4-mm facetted, 1A 11°, and turn
16	This is your middle tassel: 3A 8°, 3A 11°, 1A 4-mm square, 1A 6°, 1A 8°, 1A 11°, 4A 8°, 1A 4-mm square, 1A 6°, 3A 8°, 1B bugle, 1A 11°, 1C 3-mm square, 1A 6°, 1A 4-mm square, 3A 6°, 1A 8°, 1B facetted, 1B 11°, and turn

Now work rows 15, 14, 13, all the way back to 1, circle stitch out of the same bead that the tassel is worked from, and pick up 1B and 1A. Brick into the next pocket, going back into the second bead only, Make the edging brick-stitch to the end, finishing with 2 A beads.

Now attach the other side of the fastener with the tail thread that was left, as in Step 4, page 72. Weave away any loose threads.

Combined stitches

With this project the intention is for you to be able to recap on all that has been illustrated in the book thus far. It will be easier to do if you have been completing the projects in the book in sequence.

Cleopatra
Combined stitches

This piece is slightly more challenging, because you will need to change between different stitches all the time. It is, however, well worth the effort and the end result will show you how well different stitches can blend together. The methods used

here have all been covered extensively in the previous sections. You will be using the spiral rope, brick stitch, short and long rows, increasing in brick, on the outside, and back into spiral, with a different core and broken with a big bead. You'll then go back into brick, join the rope, string the beads, and wrap. Have fun!

I have used beads of all shapes and sizes. These may vary from necklace to necklace, as often you find yourself working with whatever beads you have handy. As long as the strings of beads are all of a given length, you can vary as much as you need. The inside length of the necklace is 44 cm.

You will need

6-g A 11° seed beads

6-g B 11° seed beads

6-g C 11° seed beads

6-g D 11° seed beads (core beads)

8-g A 8° seed beads (to match above)

8-g C 8° seed beads

4-g B 6° seed beads

3-g D 6° seed beads

(you can change these around, as long as they match the rope)

T-bar

10 matching 4-mm round beads

26 matching 6-mm round beads

10 matching 8-mm round beads

12 assorted shaped beads

Nymo B-thread

#11 or 12 beading needle

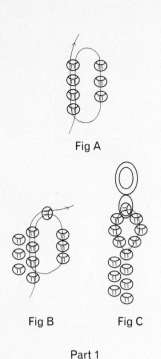

Fig A

Fig B   Fig C

Part 1

Part 1

Start with the rope at the back and work your way to the front. Thread up with a good long thread, I find 2,5 m perfect, but any longer than this and it will tangle. Spiral rope as in Method 1 (see page 36):

1 Pick up 4D 11° (core) and 3A (spiral), and thread back up the core beads (Fig A).

2 Pick up 1D 11° and 3B 11°, and thread back up the 4 core beads. (Fig B)

3 Pick up 1D 11° and 3C 11°, and thread back up the 4 core beads.

4 Pick up 1D 11° and 3A 11°, and thread back up 4 core beads.

5 Repeat 2 to 4, until you have 12 A spirals, or 34 spirals altogether (each set of three beads, counts as one spiral). End on an A spiral.

Unthread your needle, as you will now attach your clasp. Go back and thread the tail end. Pick up 7A 11° beads, and the clasp (if you are using a small clasp you will need to use 6A 14° beads). Now back through the first bead (a bead that you picked up), this will make a loop (Fig C). Take the needle up 4 core beads, turn back down the spiral, and through all the loop beads again and back up the core and turn. I like to have 3 threads through my fastening. So repeat. Then knot and travel. Knot again, travel and cut.

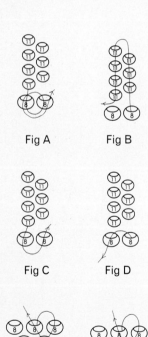

Fig A   Fig B

Fig C   Fig D

Fig E   Fig F

Brick stitch

Part 2: Brick

You will now go into the brick stitch, so go back to your thread on the working side.

1 Pick up 2A 8° beads and ladder the two together, and out of the second bead, and back up the spiral (the three beads). Turn back down the core (the 4 beads) and through the first bead. The two beads should be very secure (Fig A, B, C, D).

2 Now make an increase brick row: 3A 8° (Fig E).

3 Short row: 2A 8°.

4 Long row, increase: 3A 8° (Fig F).

5 Repeat Steps 3 and 4 until you have bricked 8 rows in all.

9 Increase row, thread is out of the end bead to start. Pick up 2A 8° and brick into the first pocket, then increase at the end, needle down 4 rows, circle stitch and out of the end bead again: 4A 8° (Fig G, H).

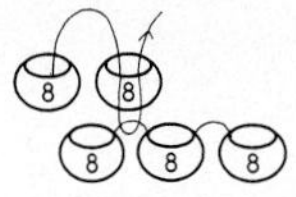

10 Increase, row: 5A 8°.

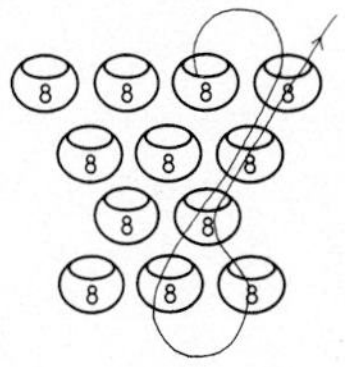

11 Increase row: 6A 8° (take the needle down 5 rows).

12 Short row: 5A 8°.

13 Long row, increase: 6A 8°.

14 Short row: 5A 8°.

15 Long Row: 6A 8°.

16 Change to a 6° bead and brick the next row. Short row: 5B 6°.

17 Long row: 6B 6°.

Make 2 of Part 1 and 2, leaving one piece to join. Now make 3 spiral ropes from the other, and start on the outer side, farthest from the neck.

Part 3: spiral ropes

First spiral rope

The core to this rope is broken with C 8° beads. It will run 2D 11°, and then 1C 8°, and continue 2D 11°, and then 1C 8° all the way.

1 To start the spiral rope thread out of the end B 6°, and pick up 1C 8°, 2D 11° (these are the core beads), 3A 11° (these are the spiral), up through the 3 core beads and back down the A-spiral (Fig A) and into the 5th bead of the brick row. Circle stitch, and out of the end bead in the brick bead row (Fig B), and up the 3 core beads, 1C 8° and 2D 11° (Fig C).

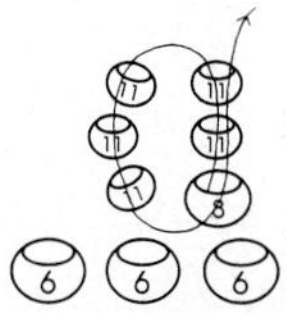

2 Pick up 1 core (1C 8°) and 3B 11°, and back up 4 core beads: 1C 8°, 2D 11°, 1C 8°.

3 Pick up 1D 11°, 3C 11°, and back through the 4 core beads.

4 Pick up 1D 11°, 3A 11°, and back through the 4 core beads.

5 Pick up 1C 8°, 3B 11°, and back through the 4 core beads.

Fig G

Fig H

Brick stitch

Fig A

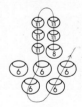

Fig B

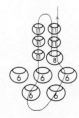

Fig C

First spiral rope

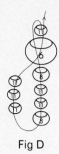

Fig D

Fig E

Fig F

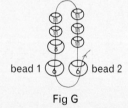

Fig G

First spiral rope

6 Pick up 1D 11°, 3C 11°, and back through the 4 core beads.

7 Pick up 1D 11°, 3A 11°, and back through the 4 core beads.

8 Repeat Rows 2 to 5 (First spiral rope), and then it's the break.

12 Pick up 1C 6-mm round, 1 core in D, turn back over the core bead and enter the 6-mm C and 4 more core beads (1C 8°, 2D 11°, and 1C 8°) and turn again back up the B spiral and through the 6-mm C and D 11° (Fig D).

13 Now continue with the rope. Pick up 1D 11°, 1C 8° (core), 3C 11°, and back through the 3 core beads (Fig E).

14 Pick up 1D 11°, 3A 11°, and back up 4 core beads (2D 11°, 1C 8°, 1D11°).

15 Pick up 1D 11°, 3B 11° and through the 4 core beads.

16 Pick up 1C 8°, 3C 11° and through the 4 core beads.

17 Pick up 1D 11°, 3A 11° and through the 4 core beads.

18 Pick up 1D11°, 3B 11°, and through the 4 core beads.

19 Pick up 1C 8°, 3C 11°, and back through the 4 core beads. You now have 18 spirals.

20 Now make the brick to which the ropes are attached, using D 6°. With the thread coming out of the C 8° bead, pick up 2D 6° and ladder them together (Fig F).

21 Now work back down the spiral, then up the core and into the new 6° bead. This will be the 1st outer bead. Work back into the 2nd bead, repeat to strengthen. Then add 2D 6°, laddered together to the base row, so there are 4D 6°. The needle should be out of the 4th bead pointing up into the work (Fig A, page 81).

Middle spiral rope

This is worked from the bottom to the top, to avoid all the joining of threads.

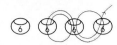

Fig A

22 Pick up 1D 11°, 1C 8°, 1D 11°, 3B, and push the beads down to the base brick and back up through the core beads and then turn down through the spiral beads, and into the 3rd bead of the base row and back round out of the 4th base bead. Repeat to strengthen as in First spiral rope (Fig E, G, page 80).

You are now ready to continue the rope,

23 Pick up 1D 11°, 3A 11°, and back up the core (1D 11°, 1C 8°, 2D 11°).

24 Pick up 1C 8°, 3C 11°, and back up the core (1C 8°, 2D 11°, 1C 8°).

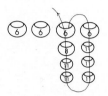

Fig B

25 Pick up 1D 11°, 3B 11°, and back up the core (2D 11°, 1C 8°, 1D 11°).

26 Repeat 23, 24, 25, 23, 24.

31 Pick up 1A 6-mm round and 1D 11°, and back through the 6-mm round, and back through the 4 core beads. Turn, through the spiral C, and make your way to the head where you left off, as for First spiral rope, Row 12.

32 Pick up 1D 11°, 1C 8°, 3B 11°, and back up the core (2D 11°, 1C 8° = 3 core).

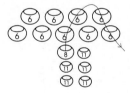

Fig C

33 Pick up 1D 11°, 3A 11°, and through 2D 11°, 1C 8°, 1D 11° = 4 core.

34 Pick up 1D 11°, 3C 11°, and through 1D 11°, 1C 8°, 2D 11°.

Middle spiral rope

35 Pick up 1C 8°, 3B 11°, and through 1C 8°, 2D 11°, 1C 8°.

36 Repeat 33, 34, 35.

39 Do not pick up a core, just 3A 11°, and back through the core as usual (17 spirals).

40 Join the middle spiral rope to the top brick, B. The first 2 beads of the brick have the first spiral rope coming from them. The middle spiral will be joined to beads 3 and 4. So take your needle up the 3rd bead, and back down the 4th bead, down the A spiral, and back up the core, back into the 3rd brick bead. Repeat. Having gone up the 3rd bead the second time travel back a row to come out of the 5th bead (Fig B, C).

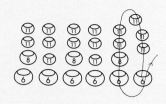

Fig A

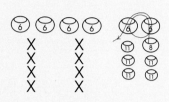

Fig B

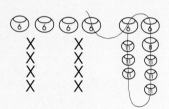

Fig C

Fig D

Fig E

Third spiral rope

Third spiral rope

41 Pick up 1C 8°, 2D 11° (core), 3A 11°, and back through the 3 core beads, and down the spiral and into the 6th brick bead B, and back out of the 5th brick bead. Repeat up the core and down the spiral through the brick and out of the core ready to continue (Fig A).

42 Pick up 1 C8°, 3B11°, and back through the core (1C 8°, 2D 11°, 1C 8° = 4 beads).

43 Pick up 1D 11°, 3C 11°, and back through the core (2D 11°, 1C 8°, 1D 11°= 4 beads).

44 Pick up 1D 11°, 3A 11°, and back up 4 core beads.

45 Pick up 1C 8°, 3B 11° B, and back up the 4 core beads.

46 BEAD BREAK: pick up 1B 6-mm round, and 1D 11°, and then take your thread over D, and back through B, and through 4 of the core beads, then turn up the B spiral, back through B 6-mm and out of the little D bead.

47 Continue, pick up 1D 11°, 1C 8° (core), 3C 11°, and back through the core (2D11°, 1C 8° = 3 beads).

48 Pick up 1D 11°, 3A 11°, and back through the 4 core beads.

49 Pick up 1D 11°, 3B 11° , and back through the 4 core beads.

50 Pick up 1C 8°, 3C 11°, and back through the 4 core beads.

51 Repeat: 48, 49, 50, 48, 49, 50, 48 (16 spirals).

58 To join to the brick, pick up 2D 6°, and ladder stitch together (Fig B, C), and then back up the A spiral, and down the 4 core beads again and into the bead on the right, up the bead on the left, and ladder stitch the two new ones to the existing beads, so that you have a row of 6D 6° (Fig D, E).

59 With the thread coming out of the 2nd bead, brick short and long rows. Brick 1 short row: 5D 6°.

60 Change to A 6° and brick a long row; 6A 6°.

61 Brick a short row: 5A 6°.

62 Repeat 60, 61, 60.

You will need

5-g A for the outline

5-g B first colour

5-g C second colour

4 matching 4-mm round beads

3 matching 6-mm round beads

Nymo D-thread

11 or 12 beading needle

key ring

1 Start with the foundation row using a thread of about 2,5 m (Fig A). Put on a stop bead and thread on 30A (row 1 becomes rows 1 and 2). See peyote on graph (page 96).

Fig A

STEP	PICK-UP
3	2A, 5B, 2A, 5C, 1A
4	2A, 4C, 1A, 1C, 1A, 4B, 1A, 1C
5	1A, 1C, 1A, 3B, 1A, 2C, 1A, 3C, 1A, 1B
6	1A, 1B, 1A, 2C, 1A, 3C, 1A, 2B, 1A, 2C
7	1A, 2C, 1A, 1B, 2A, 2C, 2A, 1C, 1A, 2B
8	1A, 2B, 2A, 1B, 1A, 1C, 1A, 1B, 2A, 3C
9	1A, 3C, 1A, 2B, 2A, 2B, 1A, 3B
10	1A, 3B, 1A, 2B, 1A, 2B, 1A, 2C, 1B, 1C
11	1A, 1C, 1B, 2C, 1A, 1B, 2A, 1B, 1A, 2B, 1C, 1B
12	1A, 1B, 1C, 2B, 2A, 1C, 2A, 2C, 2B, 1C
13	1A, 1C, 2B, 2C, 1A, 2C, 1A, 2B, 2C, 1B
14	1A, 1B, 1C, 2B, 2A, 1C, 2A, 2C, 2B, 1C
15	1A, 1C, 1B, 2C, 1A, 1C, 2A, 1B, 1A, 2B, 1C, 1B
16	1A, 3B, 1A, 2B, 1A, 2C, 1A, 2C, 1B, 1C
17	1A, 3C, 1A, 3C, 3B, 1A, 3B
18	1A, 2B, 1A, 3B, 4C, 1A, 3C
19	1A, 2C, 1A, 3C, 2A, 3B, 1A, 2B
20	1A, 1B, 1A, 3B, 3A, 3C, 1A, 2C
21	1A, 1C, 1A, 3C, 2A, 1C, 1A, 3B, 1A, 1B
22	2A, 3B, 1A, 1C, 1A, 1B, 1A, 3C, 1A, 1C

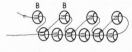

Row 2

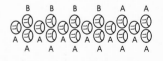

Row 3

STEP	PICK-UP
23	2A, 3C, 1A, 1B, 1A, 2C, 1A, 3B, 1A
24	1A, 3B, 1A, 1C, 1B, 1A, 2B, 1A, 3C, 1A
25	1A, 3C, 1A, 1B, 1C, 1A, 2C, 1A, 3B, 1A
26	2A, 3B, 1A, 1C, 1A, 2B, 1A, 3C, 1A
27	2A, 3C, 1A, 1B, 1A, 1C, 1A, 3B, 1A, 1C
28	1A, 1C, 1A, 3B, 2A, 1B, 1A, 3C, 1A, 1B
29	1A, 1B, 1A, 3C, 3A, 3B, 1A, 2C
30	1A, 2C, 1A, 3B, 2A, 3C, 1A, 2B

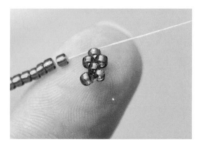

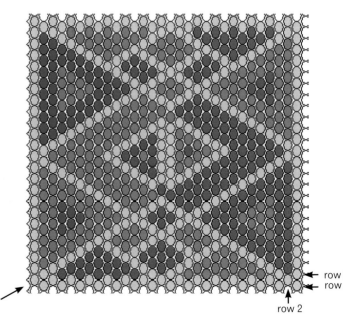

start

→ row 3
→ row 1

↑ row 2

STEP	PICK-UP
31	1A, 2B, 1A, 3C, 4B, 1A, 3C
32	1A, 3C, 1A, 3B, 3C, 1A, 3B
33	1A, 3B, 1A, 2C, 1A, 2B, 1A, 2C, 1B, 1C
34	1A, 1C, 1B, 2C, 1A, 1B, 2A, 1C, 1A, 2B, 1C, 1B
35	1A, 1B, 1C, 2B, 2A, 1B, 2A, 2C, 2B, 1C
36	1A, 1C, 2B, 2C, 1A, 2B, 1A, 2B, 2C, 1B
37	1A, 1B, 1C, 2B, 2A, 1B, 2A, 2C, 2B, 1C
38	1A, 1C, 1B, 2C, 1A, 1C, 2A, 1C, 1A, 2B, 1C, 1B
39	1A, 3B, 1A, 2C, 1A, 2C, 1A, 2C, 1B, 1C
40	1A, 3C, 1A, 2C, 2A, 2C, 1A, 3B
41	1A, 2B, 2A, 1C, 1A, 1B, 1A, 1C, 2A, 3C
42	1A, 2C, 1A, 1B, 2A, 2B, 2A, 1C, 1A, 2B
43	1A, 1B, 1A, 2C, 1A, 3B, 1A, 2B, 1A, 2C
44	1A, 1C, 1A, 3B, 1A, 2B, 1A, 3C, 1A, 1B
45	2A, 4C, 1A, 1B, 1A, 4B, 1A, 1C
46	2A, 5B, 2A, 5C, 1A
47	all A
48	all A

Fig A

Finish the key ring by picking up a 4-mm round, a 6-mm round and 1B 11° bead. Take the needle over the 11° bead and back through the 6-mm round, the 4-mm round, and through the same bead you came out of in the body of your work. Travel back a few rows and then circle stitch; back out of the other corner bead, through all the end beads again; then back into the body of the peyote. You have made the tail piece (Fig A).

TO MAKE THE TOP, take the thread up to the top bead on the other corner of your beadwork. Coming out of the top bead, pick up a 4-mm, a6-mm, another 4-mm, a 6-mm, and the last 4-mm round bead, followed by 9B 11° beads. Pick up the key ring and take the seed beads over the key ring and back down all the round beads. This forms a loop with the key ring attached (Fig B). Now work back into the body of your beadwork, circle stitch and back up all the big beads and the loop to strengthen. I like to repeat this until I have 3 threads running through the loop. Work the thread into the body, knot, travel, and cut.

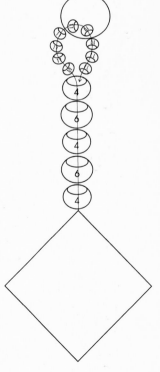

Fig B

Betty

Key ring: odd-count flat peyote

This piece is worked in odd-count flat peyote. It's a very useful stitch to know, as so often when shaping something you end up with an odd count, and struggle or wonder how to make the turn. This small key ring is perfect to help you become familiar with the technique. The advantage of this method is that it allows you to work from a centre point when creating a design.

The start of the outside rows is the same as for even-count peyote. Only the ends of the outside rows have the turn and the many threads. The piece is made up with inside rows and outside rows, or short rows and long rows. Again, for best results use Japanese beads that are regular and have a good sized hole. I have used four colours in this piece.

You will need

295A 11° seed beads for outside and lines
260B 11° seed beads for background colour
55C 11° seed beads for four smaller centre pieces
115D 11° seed beads for five larger centre pieces
4 matching 4-mm round beads
3 matching 6-mm round beads
Nymo D-thread
#11 or 12 beading needle
key ring

start

Thread your needle with about 2 m of thread, and put on a stop bead.

1 Pick up 29A (Fig A).

2 OUTSIDE ROW: pick up 1A, 6B, 1A, 6B, and 1A. Turn on the end bead as it is an outside row: 15 Beads. See Fig B, C, D, E, or go back to the section on odd-count peyote if you're not sure (see page 90). *Make the turn on all outside rows.*

3 INSIDE ROW: the end bead is there already, so the first bead will be the 2nd bead looking at your work. The last bead will be inside the last bead A on all inside rows. Pick up 14B (Fig F).

Fig A

Fig B

Fig C

Fig D

Fig B, row 2

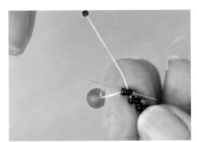

Fig D, row 2

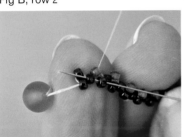

Fig D, row 2

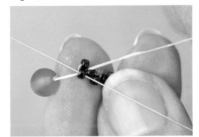

1st bead, row 2

Fig E

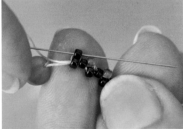

Fig E

Fig F, row 3

Fig F

Row 3

Row 3

Fig G

Fig H

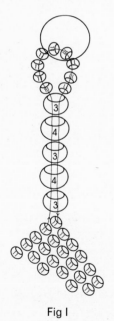

Fig I

STEP	ROW	PICK UP	BEADS
4	Outside	1A, 6B, 1A, 6B, 1A, turn (turn on all outside rows)	15
5	Inside	3B, 1A, 2B, 2A, 2B, 1A, 3B	14
6	Outside	1A, 2B, 2A, 1B, 1A, 1C, 1A, 1B, 2A, 2B, 1A	15
7	Inside	2B, 1A, 1D, 1A, 1B, 2C, 1B, 1A, 1D, 1A, 2B	14
8	Outside	1A, 2B, 2D, 1B, 1A, 1C, 1A, 1B, 2D, 2B, 1A	15
9	Inside	2B, 1A, 1D, 1A, 1B, 2C, 1B, 1A, 1D, 1A, 2B	14
10	Outside	1A, 1B, 1A, 2D, 2A, 1C, 2A, 2D, 1A, 1B, 1A	15
11	Inside	1B, 1A, 3D, 1A, 2C, 1A, 3D, 1A, 1B	14
12	Outside	1A, 1B, 4D, 1A, 1C, 1A, 4D, 1B, 1A,	15
13	Inside	1B, 1A, 3D, 1A, 2C, 1A, 3D, 1A, 1B	14
14	Outside	1A, 1B, 1A, 2D, 2A, 1C, 2A, 2D, 1A, 1B, 1A	15
15	Inside	2B, 1A, 1D, 1A, 1B, 2A, 1B, 1A, 1D, 1A, 2B	14
16	Outside	1A, 2B, 2D, 2B, 1A, 2B, 2D, 2B, 1A	15
17	Inside	2B, 1A, 1D, 1A, 1B, 2A, 1B, 1A, 1D, 1A, 2B	14
18	Outside	1A, 2B, 2A, 1B, 1A, 1D, 1A, 1B, 2A, 2B, 1A	15
19	Inside	3B, 1A, 2B, 2D, 2B, 1A, 3B	14
20	Outside	1A, 1B, 3A, 1B, 1A, 1D, 1A, 1B, 3A, 1B, 1A	15
21	Inside	1B, 2A, 1C, 2A, 2D, 2A, 1C, 2A, 1B	14
22	Outside	2A, 3C, 1A, 3D, 1A, 3C, 2A	15
23	Inside	1A, 4C, 4D, 4C, 1A	14
24	Outside	2A, 3C, 1A, 3D, 1A, 3C, 2A	15
25	Inside	1B, 2A, 1C, 2A, 2D, 2A, 1C, 2A, 1B	14
26	Outside	1A, 1B, 3A, 1B, 1A, 1D, 1A, 1B, 3A, 1B, 1A	15
27	Inside	3B, 1A, 2B, 2D, 2B, 1A, 3B	14
28	Outside	1A, 2B, 2A, 1B, 1A, 1D, 1A, 1B, 2A, 2B, 1A	15
29	Inside	2B, 1A, 1D, 1A, 1B, 2A, 1B, 1A, 1D, 1A, 2B	14
30	Outside	1A, 2B, 2D, 2B, 1A, 2B, 2D, 2B, 1A	15
31	Inside	2B, 1A, 1D, 1A, 1B, 2A, 1B, 1A, 1D, 1A, 2B	14
32	Outside	1A, 1B, 1A, 2D, 2A, 1C, 2A, 2D, 1A, 1B, 1A	15
33	Inside	1B, 1A, 3D, 1A, 2C, 1A, 3D, 1A, 1B	14
34	Outside	1A, 1B, 4D, 1A, 1C, 1A, 4D, 1B, 1A	15
35	Inside	1B, 1A, 3D, 1A, 2C, 1A, 3D, 1A, 1B	14
36	Outside	1A, 1B, 1A, 2D, 2A, 1C, 2A, 2D, 1A, 1B, 1A	15
37	Inside	2B, 1A, 1D, 1A, 1B, 2C, 1B, 1A, 1D, 1A, 2B	14

STEP	ROW	PICK UP	BEADS
38	Outside	1A, 2B, 2D, 1B, 1A, 1C, 1A, 1B, 2D, 2B, 1A	15
39	Inside	2B, 1A, 1D, 1A, 1B, 2C, 1B, 1A, 1D, 1A, 2B	14
40	Outside	1A, 2B, 2A, 1B, 1A, 1C, 1A, 1B, 2A, 2B, 1A	15
41	Inside	3B, 1A, 2B, 2A, 2B, 1A, 3B	14
42	Outside	1A, 6B, 1A, 6B, 1A	15
43	Inside	14B	14
44	Outside	15A	15
45	Inside	14A	14

With the main body complete, fasten the tail piece. From the last bead you worked, pick up a 4-mm, a 6 mm round, and 11° seed beads. Take your thread over the last bead, and back up through the other two beads, pull the tail up to the main body and enter the bead on the side (Fig G, H).

Travel a little, turn, and out of the last bead on the main body again; repeat the tail piece to strengthen. If it is long enough, use the tail-piece of the thread to add the key ring piece. If not, thread new thread and begin at the top bead in the main body, on the diagonal from the tail beads. Pick up a 4-mm, a 6-mm, a 4-mm, a 6-mm, a1 4-mm round, 9B 11° seed beads. Pick up the key ring and thread it onto the 9 seed beads. Take the needle back through all the big beads, making a loop for the key ring, and back into the other side of the corner bead. Travel back a little, turn and make your way back to the top. Travel up again to strengthen – I like to have 2–3 threads running through the loop at the top. Make sure you weave away all your threads (Fig I).

Mercia

Tie back: even-count flat peyote

I have used small 9° Gutermann beads for this project, as they are a little bigger than the 11° but still look delicate. The tie back is worked in even count flat peyote, using the same pattern as for the key ring on page 94–97 (Key ring Tanya), and then decreased at both ends. This is a very versatile pattern and can also be used to make a belt or even a small purse. The woven fabric has a lovely feel to it and I strongly recommend you make at least one big piece. As all the beads are one size, I have given you the colour reference only. Quantities are for one repeat.

You will need
(Gutermann seed beads)
1 tube A for the outline
2 tubes B first colour
2 tubes C second colour.
Two rings
Nymo D-thread
Beading needle # 11 or 12

Thread your needle with 2,5 m of thread, add a stop bead. Then pick up:

Fig A

1 4A, 1B, 1A, 1B. 1A, 1B, 1A, 1B, 1A, 1B, 5A, 1C, 1A, 1C, 1A, 1C, 1A, 1C, 1A, 1C, 3A (Fig A).

Now follow row 4 for Tanya (see page 94–97). Ensure all the A beads are aligned at the bottom, then continue to row 47. Repeat Rows 3 to 47 as many times as required for your your tie back. I repeated them 12 times.

To make the ends for the tie back

Having completed the patterns, ending on row 46, make a turn (Fig B). Coming out of the first proud bead (or second bead in), which should be an A bead, you will now lose one bead each row:

Fig B

1 1A, 5B, 2A, 5C, 1A (peyote odd-count turn).

2 1A, 4C, 1A, 1C, 1A, 4B, 1A (peyote even-count turn).

3 1A, 3B, 1A, 2C, 1A, 3C, 1A, turn.

4 1A, 1B, 2A, 2C, 2A, 1C, 1A, turn.

5 2A, 1B, 1A, 1C, 1A, 1B, 2A, turn.

6 1A, 2B, 2A, 2B, 1A, turn.

7 1A, 2B, 1A, 2B, 1A, turn.

8 1A, 1B, 2A, 1B, 1A, turn.

9 2A, 1C, 2A turn.

10 1A, 2C, 1A.

11 For a good point, put in 2A together, then 1C, and 2A together again.

12 Normal 1A, 1A.

13 2A together, and fasten off. Weave back into the work.

Go back and do the other end making sure that the B-beads lie on top of the B-beads, and the C-beads on top of the C-beads.
    Attach a ring to both ends on the tie back.

Sam
Wineglass marker

These little stars are lovely on their own, but used as markers on the glasses at a cocktail party or at a dinner table, they will most certainly draw comments from the guests. They start in flat circular peyote, take a little shape with some increasing, and are dead-easy to finish. You can also use sparkling colours and make them up for Christmas. I have used two sizes of beads in order to keep them flat.

You will need
95A 9° Gutermann seed beads
40B 11° seed beads
20C 11° seed beads
2 magnetic beads
Nymo D-thread
#10 or 11 beading needle

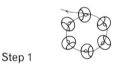

Step 1

1 Thread up with 1,5 m (it is good to try to finish this piece in one thread), and pick up 6A 9°. Tie this into a circle using a reef knot (left over right and right over left). The knot must not slip.

Step 2

2 Now pick up 1B 11°, take the needle and thread across the centre of the circle, entering the 4th bead and up the 5th and 6th bead from the thread where you started. You should have a circle with the B bead in the centre.

3 Pick up 1B 11° and go through the A bead, repeat. You will have a B in each space between the A beads: 6 beads have been added. End the row by going through the last A bead and then up through the first B bead. This brings your thread up and ready for the next row and is called a step up; you will do a step up at the end of every row.

Step 3

4 Pick up 2C 11°, and add them together between the B beads, ending through the B bead. Step up through the C (only the first one); you will be in the middle.

Step 4

5 Pick up 1C 11°, and go through the next C. The C you have added will sit on top of the 2C base to form a triangle. Then pick up 1B 11° and go through the next C bead (you will have 2B beads sitting on top of each other, and a

Step 5

Step 6

Step 7

Step 8

Step 9

triangle of C beads). Repeat to complete the row, ending with a B through C. Step up into the next C.

6 Add 1B and go through 1B. Add 1B and go through 1C, add 1B and through 1B, add 1B, and through 1C – all the way round. Finally add 1B through 1C, and step up through a B.

7 Add 1A 9°, and go through a B. The A is the outer perimeter; this bead sits in the ditch. Now add 2B together, and go through the next B bead. This is the build up of the points of the stars; they sit on top of your little C triangle. Continue, pick up 1A and go through a B, and so on. End with 2B through a B and step up to the A.

8 Pick up 1A and go through a B, pick up 1B and go through the other B (this B sits on the top of the point of the inner line in the star). Then 1A and through an A, and pick up another A, through a B. You will have 3A together, the outer line growing. End with 1A, through A, and the next A. You have stepped up.

9 Pick up an A through B at the top point, then A through 3As, then A through B. Continue, ending with A through 4As.

10 Pick up 2A together at the point and through the 5A. Repeat to the other side, ending with 2A, and through 6A.

11 Add 1A to each point, and travel down the outer 7A beads. There should be 9 beads from the point. Travel once round the outer perimeter, coming out at the point of one of the stars to make the arm. Pick up 6C 11°, 3A 9°, a magnet bead, and 1C 11°. Push the beads to the star and back over the 11° bead, through the magnetic bead, 9 seed beads, and through the point bead of the star. Make the other arm to match the first, then back into the star and weave away the thread. These little arms will wrap around the stem of the glass.

Step 10

Sebastian

Little egg basket

This project is worked using flat circular peyote; with increasing within a row.

These little baskets are pure fun and can be used for whatever you can imagine! Fill them with tiny chocolate eggs for Easter or give them to someone special as a small birthday gift. They're guaranteed to bring a smile to any person's face.

I have used 9° Gutermann seed beads. You will start with the flat circular peyote, and then change to even count circular peyote for the walls, increasing at the same time. I have used only 3 colours, because this makes it easier to see with which row you are working. I like to use Monofil because the thread is practically invisible. I also find it stiffens the basket a little.

You will need
(Gutermann seed beads)
263 A 9° for basket, top and handle
249 B 9° for basket
306 C 9° for basket and handle
extra beads to make the flowers
7 m Monofil 40 Madeira (or Monofil 330 Denier – this is a little heavier than
the 40 Maderia, and gives it the stiffness needed)
11 beading needle (or #10 for the Denier)
8 x 8-cm-square of cellophane to line the basket
mini chocolate eggs

Fig A

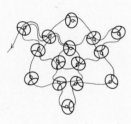

Fig B

Fig C

You will start with the base and increase within the rows. To increase is to pick up two beads together and place them into the space; the next row you will work an extra bead.

1 Thread up with about 2,5 m of Monofil and pick up 3A, then tie these into a circle with a reef knot (left over right and right over left). Take your needle through the first bead to the left. You will be sewing anti-clockwise if you are right handed and clockwise if you are left handed (Fig A).

2 You will now increase in each space: pick up 2B, and go into the next bead, 3 times. You will have 6 beads, now step up. Having gone through the last A, now step up to the first B bead of the row you have just completed. You will do this at the end of every row. Step up (Fig B).

3 Pick up (1C and go through a B bead) 6 times, and then step up, through a B, and then the first C bead: 6C beads have been put in (Fig C). It is very important to keep a watch on how many beads at the end of every row, because as soon as you are out it won't work. A tip is to count out the number of beads to use first and put them in front of you).

4 Increase row: pick up (2A together, and go through a C) 6 times: 12A beads have been added. Step up, through the last C and the first A.

5 Normal row: pick up (1B and go through an A) 12 times: 12B beads have been added. Step up.

6 Increase row: pick up (2C together and go through a B). Then pick up (1C and go through a B) twice. Repeat this step 3 times: 16C beads. Step up.

7 Normal row: pick up (1A and go through a C) 16 times: 16A beads. Step up.

8 Increase row: pick up (1B and go through an A) 3 times and then increase, (pick up two beads together). Repeat this step 3 times: 20B beads. Step up.

9 Normal row: pick up (1C and go through a B) 20 times: 20C beads. Step up.

10 Normal row: pick up (1A and go through a C) 20 times: 20A beads. Step up.

11 Normal row: pick up (1B and go through an A) 20 times: 20B beads.

Step up. Keep the tension tight and even here as this is the start of the walls.

12 Increase row: pick up (1C and go through a B) twice and then increase (pick up two C beads together). Now pick up (1C and go into a B) 4 times and then increase. Again, pick up (1C and go into a B) 4 times and then increase. One last time, pick up (1C and go into a B) 4 times and then increase. End with (1C and through a B) twice, and step up: 24 C beads.

13 Normal row: pick up (1A and go through a C) 24 times: 24A beads, step up.

14 Normal row: pick up (1B and go through an A) 24 times: 24B beads. Step up.

15 Increase row: pick up (1C and go through a B), and then increase. [Pick up (1C and go through a B) 5 times and then increase] 3 times. Pick up (1C and go through a B) 4 times: 28 C beads. Step up.

16 Normal row: pick up (1A and go through a C) 28 times: 28A beads. Step up.

17 Normal row: pick up (1B and go through an A) 28 times: 28B beads. Step up.

18 Normal row: pick up (1C and go through a B) 28 times: 28C beads. Step up.

19 Normal row: pick up (1A and go through a C) 28 times: 28A beads. Step up.

20 Normal row: pick up (1B and go through an A) 28 times: 28B beads. Step up.

21 Increase row: pick up (1C and go through a B) 5 times and then increase. Now [pick up (1C and go through a B) 6 times, and then increase] 3 times. Pick up 1C and go through a B: 32C beads. Step up.

22 Normal row: pick up (1A and through a C) 32 times: 32A beads, Step up.

23 Normal row: pick up (1B and go through an A) 32 times: 32B beads. Step up.

24 Increase row: pick up (1C and go through a B) 4 times, and then increase. [Pick up (1 C and go through a B) 7 times, and then increase] twice. Pick up (1C and through a B) 3 times: 36C beads. Step up.

25 Normal row: pick up (1A and go through a C) 36 times: 36A beads. Step up.

26 Normal row: pick up (1B and go through an A) 36 times: 36B beads. Step up.

27 Increase row: pick up (1C and go through a B) 3 times, and then increase. [Pick up (1C and go through a B) 8 times, and then increase] twice. Pick up (1C and through a B) 5 times: 40C beads. Step up.

28 Normal row: pick up (1A and go through a C) 40 times: 40A beads.

To make the handle

Put in a new thread and come out at the centre point of one of the side walls. Count in 5A-beads from the corner, and come out of the C bead to the left in the row below, the needle facing out (Fig A).

Fig A

1 Pick up 1C and turn the needle through A and C to the right (Fig B). You pick up one bead and go through two beads.

2 Turn again and pick up 1C and 1A, and needle through the C bead you have just put on. You pick up two beads and go through one bead (Fig C).

Fig B

These two rows make the handle. Repeat until you have 27C beads on row 1 and 26C beads on row 2. Join the handle out of row 1, through A and C in the basket centre on the other side, and back through A and C in the handle. Weave in and out to strengthen.

You will then strengthen the entire handle with ladder stitch, treating the three beads as one, in a row.

Fig C

To make the little flower

Come out of the centre bead in the handle and pick up 6 beads in any colour. Take the beads to the basket, and go back through the first bead to form a loop. Enter the basket through the same bead you came out of, bringing the loop (or flower) close, snug up to the basket (Fig D). Make another flower from the same beads. I made 3 to 5 on each side, and four on the top of the handle. Work from one side to the other.

Fig D

To finish off the top edge

Once your handle is on with the flowers, come out of the A bead next to the handle. Pick up (1C and go through A) 3 times, then increase. Pick up (1C and go through A) 4 times, and increase. Pick up (1C go through A) 4 times, and increase. Pick up (1C go through A) 4 times, and through the handle. Now, out of the A bead next to the handle on the other side, pick up (1C and go through A) 3 times, then increase, and pick up (1C and go through A) 4 times, and increase. Pick up (1C and go through A) 4 times, and increase. This is the last corner. Pick up (1C and go through A) 4 times. Join up with the handle. Your top now matches the handle.

To stiffen the handle a little more, give it 2 coats of clear nail varnish, letting the coats dry in between applications. You may want give the base a coat as well.

Yvonne

Peyote odd count necklace

Odd count tubular peyote is another very versatile stitch. Because the tube is hollow, you can thread it with wire or cord and make all kinds of interesting things. I have chosen to make a necklace. I have started with a very simple piece (Part 1), which is ideal for beginners and can be made into a necklace on its own. In Part 2 I add another bead and Part 3 makes up most of the necklace. The aim is to show you how different beads can be mixed.

You will need
1-g 14° for the fastener
6-g A 11° leader
8-g C 11° dominant colour
6-g B 11° second colour
8-g A 8° dominant colour
8-g C baby drops
Nymo D-thread
3 each A, B, C 6-mm round beads for tassel
#10 or 11 beading needle
fastener

Part 1

ROW ONE

1 Thread up about 2 m of thread and leave a tail of about 20 to 30cm. Pick up 1A, 2C, 2B, 2C, all 11° seed beads. Make a circle, tie into a knot (reef knot. left over right and right over left). The knot must not slip, for it will be very difficult to work. Test your circle, if it does slip, tie again. Hold the tail firmly in your hand (Fig A).

ROW TWO

2 Take your needle through A, travelling to the left (anti-clockwise).
To make this pattern, the colour you come out of is the colour you pick up all the time. So pick up 1A and take the needle through the second C bead on the circle (Fig B).

Always use the longest string of thread you can handle, as every time you put in a new thread, you create a weak spot.

3 Pick up 1C, and go through the 2nd B bead. Note that you are picking up the colour you came out of (Fig C).

4 Pick up 1B and go through the 2nd C bead (Fig D).

5 Pick up 1C and go through the 2nd A. This was the first bead of the second row (Fig E).

You have just completed the second row. If you wish, now is a good time to put a toothpick or a small knitting needle through the centre of the circle. Pull up the thread – there should be 4 beads that stand up (C, B, C, A.). You will now work through these 4 beads in turn (Fig E).

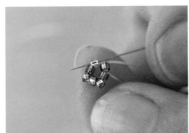

Fig A

Fig B

Fig C

Fig D

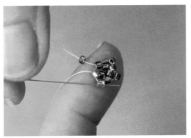

Fig E

Row 1

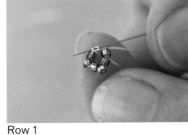

Row 1

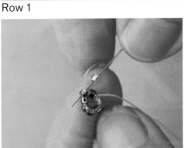

Row 2, Step 2

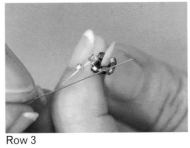

Row 2, Step 3

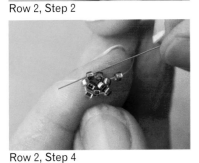

Row 2, Step 4

Row 2, Step 5

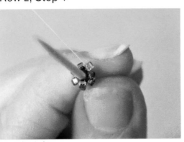

Toothpick

Row 3

Row three

6 Pick up 1A and go through the 2nd C, which is one of the 4 beads that stood up in Step 5.

7 Pick up 1C and go through the 2nd B that stood up in Step 5.

8 Pick up 1B and go through the 2nd C that stood up in Step 5.

9 Pick up 1C and go through the A you started the row with (2nd A).

10 Your spiralling has begun and you will continue in this manner with 18 repetitions from Row 3, Steps 6 to 9. You will have done 21 rows. This will give you a small piece of spiral rope using just 11° seed beads. In Part 2, I introduce the drops.

Note: I personally don't like to keep the toothpick or knitting needle in for too long, as I feel it affects the tension. Do keep your eye on this.

Part 2

Continue in the same manner still going through every second bead.

1 Pick up 1A and go through the C.

2 Pick up 1C and go through the B.

3 Pick up 1B and go through the C.

Part 2, Step 4

Part 2, Step 5

Part 2, Step 6

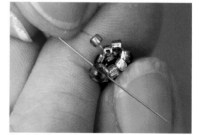

Part 2, Step 7

4 Now the drop. Pick up a drop in C (instead of the seed bead) and go through A.

5 Pick up 1A, and go through C.

6 Pick up 1C and go through B,

7 Pick up 1B and go through the C drop,

8 Pick up 1little C bead and go through A

9 Now repeat Part 2, Steps 1 to 8 until you have added 12 drops, ending with Step 4.

Part 3

You will now add the 8° seed beads to finish with a necklace made using a combination of three bead sizes.

1 Pick up 1C drop go through A.

2 Pick up 1A go through C.

3 Pick up 1C go through B.

4 Pick up 1B go through 1C drop.

5 Pick up a C seed bead and go through the A seed bead.

6 Pick up 1A 8° and go through C.

7 Pick up 1C go through B.

8 Pick up 1B take it over the C drop and through the little C.

9 Pick up 1C drop and go through big A.

10 Pick up 1A 8° bead and go through C.

11 Pick up 1C and go through 1B.

12 Pick up 1B and go through the C drop.

13 Pick up 1C and go through the A 8° seed bead

14 Repeat from 6 to 13 for as long as you wish. I put in 59A 8° beads and 140 drops in total.

Having put in the 59A 8° beads, revert back to *Part 2* and leave out the 8° beads. Put in only the drops, until you have put in 140 drops.

To complete the necklace, go back to *Part 1* and finish with the spiral, using no big beads, to match the first half.

To attach the fastenings, tidy the ends, thread up with the tail, and go through the end proud beads bringing them together twice. Then pick up 4C 14°, pick up the lobster claw, or whatever fastener you have, and go through the ring on the end, then pick up the 3 remaining 14° seed beads and go through the first 14° bead you picked up – needle heading towards your work. And finally, go through the other side of the tube, so that the fastening sits centrally. Repeat twice more so that there are three threads running through the fastening for strength.

Do the same on the other side, putting on the ring.

Part 2, Step 8

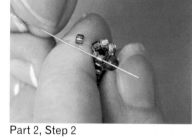
Part 2, Step 2

Part 3, Step 1

Part 3, Step 6

Part 3, Step 1

Result

To make the tassel

Thread up with a good long thread, leaving a tail of about 30cm.

1 Pick up 2 beads in 11° C and go round in a circle and back up the first bead (Fig A).

2 Pick up two more beads and down the second bead (the 2 beads should sit on top of the 2 beads already there), and go back up the first bead and new bead (Fig B, C).

3 Pick up 2 beads again in the main colour C, and go down 2 beads, then back up 3 beads. Continue with step 3 until you have 22 rows (Fig D, E).

4 Now pick up a 1C 6-mm round bead, 2C 11° C, and turn back down the 6-mm and 2 more C 11° on the stem. Go back up the other half of the stem, back through the 6-mm and one of the two beads on the end, after the big bead (Fig F, G). And continue …

5 Pick up 2 more C 11° beads, down the one bead and up 2.

Fig A

Fig B

Fig C

Fig D

Fig E

Fig F

Fig G

Tassel Step 1

Tassel Step 2

Tassel Step 2

Tassel Step 3

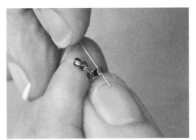
Tassel Step 3

Continue

6 Repeat Row 3 until you have completed 20 rows.

This is the stem and loop from which the tassels will hang

7 Come out of the bottom of the stem and add 4C 11°, 1A 8°, 1B 11°, 1C 11°, and 1B 6-mm round bead and 1 14°. Turn back over the little 14°, and up the large round bead and all the others up to the stem, and up another 2 beads on the stem (the same ones you came out of). Turn and go down the sister bead, out to the bottom of the stem, ready for the next tassel (Fig H).

8 TASSEL 2: Pick up 4B 11°, 1A 8°, 1C 11°, 1C 6-mm round bead, and 1C 14°. Thread over the little 14° and back up all the beads to the top of the tassel, and up two more rows in the stem, out and ready to start the next tassel.

9 TASSEL 3: Pick up 4A 11°, 1A 8°, 1B 11°, 1C 6-mm round bead, and 1C 14°. Turn and go back over the little 14°, and up all the tassel beads, and two more in the stem. Turn and go down the two sister beads next to it, ready for the next tassel (Fig I).

10 TASSEL 4: Pick up 4B 11°, 1A 8°, 1C 11°, 1B 11°, and 1A 6-mm round bead, and 1C 14°. Turn and go up all the beads as before, and the 2 more rows in the stem ready for the next tassel.

11 TASSEL 5: Pick up 4C 11°, 1A 8°, 2C 11°, 1B 6-mm round bead, and 1C 14°. Turn back up all the beads, and two more in the stem. Turn down the sister bead, ready for the 6th tassel.

12 TASSEL 6: Pick up 4B 11°, 1A 8°, 1B 11°, 1A 6-mm round bead, and 1C 14°bead. Turn back up all the beads, and two more in the stem.

13 TASSEL 7: Pick up 4B 11°, 1A 8°, 1B 11°, 1A 6-mm round bead, and the 14° bead. Turn up all the beads, and 2 more in the stem. Turn and go down the 2 sister beads, ready for the next tassel .

14 TASSEL 8: This is the last of the big beads. Pick up 4c 11°, 1A 8°, 1B 11°, 1B 6-mm round bead, and the 14°. Turn up all the beads in the tassel, and 2 more, ready for the next tassel.

15 TASSEL 9: Pick up 4A 11°, 1A 8°, 1C 11°, 1A 11°, followed by a drop, and then back up the beads to the top of the tassel, and 2 more in the stem. Turn down the 2 sister beads, ready for the next tassel.

16 TASSEL 10: Pick up 4B 11°, 1A 8°, 2C 11°, followed by a drop. Go back up to the top of the tassel, and 2 more beads in the stem.

17 TASSEL 11: Pick up 4C 11°, 1A 8°, 1C 11°, 1A 11°, and a drop. Work back up the tassel.

Fig H

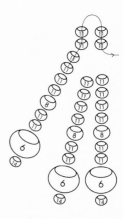

Fig I

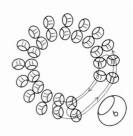

Fig J

18 Repeat the colours of 15, 16, and 17 until 12 little tassels have been made. There should be 20 tassels in total.

To close the top

Thread up with the tail thread and bring the loop round to meet the stem above the 6-mm bead. Take the needle through the two beads on the same side as the thread, the needle going from the big bead and up two beads. Then work down the 2 sister beads on top of the big bead, and back up the two beads on the same side as the thread on the first piece (the last bead is unattached). Repeat to strengthen, take the thread down the stem and cut off (Fig J, page 119).

To put in a new thread

Try to finish the old thread after an A bead and knot. Unthread the needle and leave. Thread up with new thread and weave it into the peyote, exiting where the old thread was left. Pick up the next bead, knot again, and continue as usual. Having grown the piece a little, weave the old thread away into the new work.

Thandi
Table mat

This project is worked in two-drop even-count peyote. It is made using the same method as was used to make the key ring, but instead of picking up one bead and going through one bead, you will pick up two beads at a time and go through two beads. The mat I have chosen to make has an African feel, and I thought it would be a good way to end the projects in this book. Beads have a long history in Africa and I am proud to live in this beautiful and diverse land.

The mat is made using 8° seed beads. They are irregular, making it a little more difficult to get an even surface. The graph shows you rows 1 to 64; use rows 5 to 64 to repeat the pattern as many times as you need. The number of beads is for one repeat, so multiply the beads by the number of repeats.

You will need
1 505 A 8° background
755 B 8° outline
410 C 8° dark (black)
162 D 8° colour 1 (green)
340 E 8° main colour in pattern (rust)
162 F 8° colour 2 (gold)
60 G 8° colour 3 (clear tint)
Nymo B-thread
#10 or 11 beading needle

1 Thread up with about 2,5 m of single thread and pick up 104A. Use double thread if you are in doubt about the strength of the thread.

2 Pick up 2A, and through 2A. Pick up 2A and go through 2A. Continue all the way back to the beginning. Your last step is going through 2A: 52 beads. *There should be 52 beads at the end of each row throughout.*

STEP	PICK UP
3	2A, 2B, 2C, 2C, 2B, 2B, 2B, 2C, 2C, 2B, 2B, 2B, 2C, 2C, 2B, 2B, 2B, 2C, 2C, 2B, 2B, 2B, 2C, 2C, 2B, and lastly 2B
4	2A, 2A, (1D+1C), 2E, (1C+1D), 2A, 2A, (1F+1C), 2E, (1C+1F), 2A, 2A, (1E+1C), 2E, (1C+1E), 2A, 2A, (1D+1C), 2E, (1C+1D), 2A, 2A, (1F+1C), 2E, (1C+1F), 2A
5	2A, (1B+1F), (1C+1A), (1A+1C), (1F+1B), 2A, (1B+1D), (1C+1A), (1A+1C), (1D+1B), 2A, (1B+1E), (1C+1A), (1A+1C), (1E+1B), 2A, (1B+1F), (1C+1A), (1A+1C), (1F+1B), 2A, (1B+1D), (1C+1A), (1A+1C), (1D+1B), 2A
6	2A, (1A+1B), 2C, 2E, 2C, (1B+1A), (1A+1B), 2C, 2E, 2C, (1B+1A), (1A+1B), 2C, 2E, 2C, (1B+1A), (1A+1B), 2C, 2E, 2C, (1B+1A), (1A+1B), 2C, 2E, 2C, (1B+1A)
7	2A, 2F, 2A, 2A, 2F, 2A, 2D, 2A, 2A, 2D, 2A, 2E, 2A, 2A, 2E, 2A, 2F, 2A, 2A, 2F, 2A, 2D, 2A, 2A, 2D, 2A
8	2A, 2B, 2C, 2A, 2C, 2B, 2B, 2C, 2A, 2C, 2B, 2B, 2C, 2A, 2C, 2B, 2B, 2C, 2A, 2C, 2B, 2B, 2C, 2A, 2C, 2B
9	2A, 2F, 2A, 2A, 2F, 2A, 2D, 2A, 2A, 2D, 2A, 2E, 2A, 2A, 2E, 2A, 2F, 2A, 2A, 2F, 2A, 2D, 2A, 2A, 2D, 2A
10	2A, (1B+1D), (1C+1A), 2A, (1A+1C), (1D+1B), (1B+1F), (1C+1A), 2A, (1A+1C), (1F+1B), (1B+1E), (1C+1A), 2A, (1A+1C), (1E+1B), (1B+1D), (1C+1A), 2A, (1A+1C), (1D+1B), (1B+1F), (1C+1A), 2A, (1A+1C), (1F+1B)
11	2A, 2F, 2A, 2A, 2F, 2A, 2D, 2A, 2A, 2D, 2A, 2E, 2A, 2A, 2E, 2A, 2F, 2A, 2A, 2F, 2A, 2D, 2A, 2A, 2D, 2A
12	2A, (B+D), (C+A), 2A, (A+C), (D+B), (B+F), (C+A), 2A, (A+C), (F+B), (B+E), (C+A), 2A, (A+C), (E+B), (B+D), (C+A), 2A, (A+C), (D+B), (B+F), (C+A), 2A, (A+C), (F+B)
13	2A, 2F, 2A, 2A, 2F, 2A, 2D, 2A, 2A, 2D, 2A, 2E, 2A, 2A, 2E, 2A, 2F, 2A, 2A, 2F, 2A, 2D, 2A, 2A, 2D, 2A
14	2A, 2B, (D+C), 2A, (C+D), 2B, 2B, (F+C), 2A, (C+F), 2B, 2B, (E+C), 2A, (C+E), 2B, 2B, (D+C), 2A, (C+D), 2B, 2B, (F+C), 2A, (C+F), 2B
15	2A, (B+F), (C+A), (A+C), (F+B), 2A, (B+D), (C+A), (A+C), (D+B), 2A, (B+E), (C+A), (A+C), (E+B), 2A, (B+F), (C+A), (A+C), (F+B), 2A, (B+D), (C+A), (A+C), (D+B), 2A

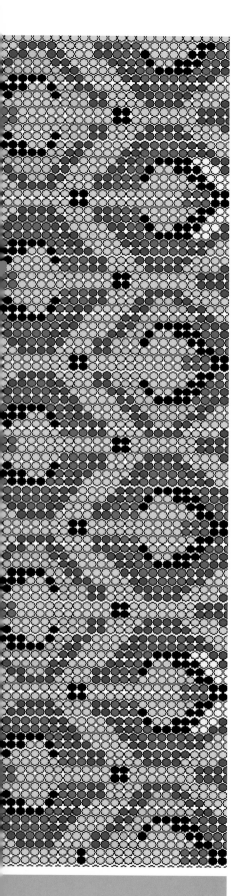

STEP	PICK UP
16	2A, (A+B), 2D, 2A, 2D, (B+A), (A+B), 2F, 2A, 2F, (B+A), (A+B), 2E, 2A, 2E, (B+A), (A+B), 2D, 2A, 2D, (B+A), (A+B), 2F, 2A, 2F, (B+A)
17	2A, 2B, 2F, 2F, 2B, 2A, 2B, 2D, 2D, 2B, 2A, 2B, 2E, 2E, 2B, 2A, 2B, 2F, 2F, 2B, 2A, 2B, 2D, 2D, 2B, 2A
18	2A, 2A, (B+D), 2A, (D+B), 2A, 2A, (B+F), 2A, (F+B), 2A, 2A, (B+E), 2A, (E+B), 2A, 2A, (B+D), 2A, (D+B), 2A, 2A, (B+F), 2A, (F+B), 2A
19	2A, (A+B), 2F, 2F, (B+A), 2C, (A+B), 2D, 2D, (B+A), 2C, (A+B), 2E, 2E, (B+A), 2C, (A+B), 2F, 2F, (B+A), 2C, (A+B), 2D, 2D, (B+A), 2A
20	2A, 2A, 2B, 2A, 2B, 2A, 2A, 2B, 2A, 2B, 2A, 2A, 2B, 2A, 2B, 2A, 2A, 2B, 2A, 2B, 2A, 2A, 2B, 2A, 2B, 2A
21	2A, 2A, 2F, 2F, 2A, 2C, 2A, 2D, 2D, 2A, 2C, 2A, 2E, 2E, 2A, 2C, 2A, 2F, 2F, 2A, 2C, 2A, 2D, 2D, 2A, 2C
22	2A, 2A, (A+B), 2A, (B+A), 2A, 2A, (A+B), 2A, (B+A), 2A, 2A, (A+B), 2A, (B+A), 2A, 2A, (A+B), 2A, (B+A), 2A, 2A, (A+B), 2A, (B+A), 2A
23	2A, 2A, 2B, 2B, 2A, 2A, 2A, 2B, 2B, 2A, 2A, 2A, 2B, 2B, 2A, 2A, 2A, 2B, 2B, 2A, 2A, 2A, 2B, 2B, 2A, 2A
24	2A, 2B, 2A, 2A, 2A, 2B, 2B, 2A, 2A, 2A, 2B, 2B, 2A, 2A, 2A, 2B, 2B, 2A, 2A, 2A, 2B, 2B, 2A, 2A, 2A, 2B
25	2A, 2A, 2B, 2B, 2A, 2A, 2A, 2B, 2B, 2A, 2A, 2A, 2B, 2B, 2A, 2A, 2A, 2B, 2B, 2A, 2A, 2A, 2B, 2B, 2A, 2A
26	2A, 2B, 2A, 2A, 2A, 2B, 2B, 2A, 2A, 2A, 2B, 2B, 2A, 2A, 2A, 2B, 2B, 2A, 2A, 2A, 2B, 2B, 2A, 2A, 2A, 2B
27	2A, (B+A), 2A, 2A, (A+B), 2A, (B+A), 2A, 2A, (A+B), 2A, (B+A), 2A, 2A, (A+B), 2A, (B+A), 2A, 2A, (A+B), 2A, (B+A), 2A, 2A, (A+B), 2A
28	2A, 2F, 2A, 2C, 2A, 2E, 2E, 2A, 2C, 2A, 2D, 2D, 2A, 2C, 2A, 2F, 2F, 2A, 2C, 2A, 2E, 2E, 2A, 2C, 2A, 2D
29	2A, 2B, 2A, 2A, 2B, 2A, 2B, 2A, 2A, 2B, 2A, 2B, 2A, 2A, 2B, 2A, 2B, 2A, 2A, 2B, 2A, 2B, 2A, 2A, 2B, 2A
30	2A, 2F, (B+A), 2C, (A+B), 2E, 2E, (B+A), 2C, (A+B), 2D, 2D, (B+A), 2C, (A+B), 2F, 2F, (B+A), 2C, (A+B), 2E, 2E, (B+A), 2C, (A+B), 2D
31	2A, (D+B), 2A, 2A, (B+E), 2A, (E+B), 2A, 2A, (B+F), 2A, (F+B), 2A, 2A, (B+D), 2A, (D+B), 2A, 2A, (B+E), 2A, (E+B), 2A, 2A, (B+F), 2A
32	2A, 2F, 2B, 2A, 2B, 2E, 2E, 2B, 2A, 2B, 2D, 2D, 2B, 2A, 2B, 2F, 2F, 2B, 2A, 2B, 2E, 2E, 2B, 2A, 2B, 2D

STEP	PICK UP
33	2A, 2D, (B+A), (A+B), 2E, 2A, 2E, (B+A), (A+B), 2F, 2A, 2F, (B+A), (A+B), 2D, 2A, 2D, (B+A), (A+B), 2E, 2A, 2E, (B+A), (A+B), 2F, 2A
34	2A, (A+C), (F+B), 2A, (B+E), (C+A), (A+C), (E+B), 2A, (B+D), (C+A), (A+C), (D+B), 2A, (B+F), (C+A), (A+C), (F+B), 2A, (B+E), (C+A), (A+C), (E+B), 2A, (B+D), (C+A)
35	2A, (C+D), 2B, 2B, (E+C), 2A, (C+E), 2B, 2B, (F+C), 2A,(C+F), 2B, 2B, (D+C), 2A, (C+D), 2B, 2B, (E+C), 2A, (C+E), 2B, 2B, (F+C), 2A
36	2A, 2A, 2F, 2A, 2E, 2A, 2A, 2E, 2A, 2D, 2A, 2A, 2D, 2A, 2F, 2A, 2A, 2F, 2A, 2E, 2A, 2A, 2E, 2A, 2D, 2A
37	2A, (A+C), (D+B), (B+E), (C+A), 2A, (A+C), (E+B), (B+F), (C+A), 2A, (A+C), (F+B), (B+D), (C+A), 2A, (A+C), (D+B), (B+E), (C+A), 2A, (A+C), (E+B), (B+F), (C+A), 2A
38	2A, 2A, 2F, 2A, 2E, 2A, 2A, 2E, 2A, 2D, 2A, 2A, 2D, 2A, 2F, 2A, 2A, 2F, 2A, 2E, 2A, 2A, 2E, 2A, 2D, 2A
39	2A, (A+C), (D+B), (B+E), (C+A), 2A, (A+C), (E+B), (B+F), (C+A), 2A, (A+C), (F+B), (B+D), (C+A), 2A, (A+C), (D+B), (B+E), (C+A), 2A, (A+C), (E+B), (B+F), (C+A), 2A
40	2A, 2A, 2F, 2A, 2E, 2A, 2A, 2E, 2A, 2D, 2A, 2A, 2D, 2A, 2F, 2A, 2A, 2F, 2A, 2E, 2A, 2A, 2E, 2A, 2D, 2A
41	2A, 2C, 2B, 2B, 2C, 2A, 2C, 2B, 2B, 2C, 2A, 2C, 2B, 2B, 2C, 2A, 2C, 2B, 2B, 2C, 2A, 2C, 2B, 2B, 2C, 2A
42	2A, 2A, 2F, 2A, 2E, 2A, 2A, 2E, 2A, 2D, 2A, 2A, 2D, 2A, 2F, 2A, 2A, 2F, 2A, 2E, 2A, 2A, 2E, 2A, 2D, 2A
43	2A, 2C, (B+A), (A+B), 2C, 2E, 2C, (B+A), (A+B), 2C, 2E, 2C, (B+A), (A+B), 2C, 2E, 2C, (B+A), (A+B), 2C, 2E, 2C, (B+A), (A+B), 2C, 2E
44	2A, (A+C), (F+B), 2A, (B+E), (C+A), (A+C), (E+B), 2A, (B+D), (C+A), (A+C), (D+B), 2A, (B+F), (C+A), (A+C), (F+B), 2A, (B+E), (C+A), (A+C), (E+B), 2A, (B+D), (C+A)
45	2A, (C+E), 2A, 2A, (G+C), 2E, (C+G), 2A, 2A, (E+C), 2E, (C+E), 2A, 2A, (E+C), 2E, (C+E), 2A, 2A, (G+C), 2E, (C+G), 2A, 2A, (E+C), 2E
46	2A, 2C, 2B, 2B, 2B, 2C, 2C, 2B, 2B, 2B, 2C, 2C, 2B, 2B, 2B, 2C, 2C, 2B, 2B, 2B, 2C, 2C, 2B, 2B, 2B, 2C
47	2A, 2E, 2A, 2A, 2G, 2E, 2G, 2A, 2A, 2E, 2E, 2E, 2A, 2A, 2E, 2E, 2E, 2A, 2A, 2G, 2E, 2G, 2A, 2A, 2E, 2E
48	2A, (C+E), (B+A), 2B, (A+B), (G+C), (C+G), (B+A), 2B, (A+B),(E+C), (C+E), (B+A), 2B, (A+B), (E+C), (C+E), B+A), 2B, (A+B), (G+C), (C+G), (B+A), 2B, (A+B), (E+C)

STEP	PICK UP
49	2A, (E+B), 2A, 2A, (B+G), 2C, (G+B), 2A, 2A, (B+E), 2C, (E+B), 2A, 2A, (B+E), 2C, (E+B), 2A, 2A, (B+G), 2C, (G+B), 2A, 2A, (B+E), 2C
50	2A, 2E, 2A, 2B, 2A, 2G, 2G, 2A, 2B, 2A, 2E, 2E, 2A, 2B, 2A, 2E, 2E, 2A, 2B, 2A, 2G, 2G, 2A, 2B, 2A, 2E
51	2A, 2B, (A+B), (B+A), 2B, 2C, 2B, (A+B), (B+A), 2B, 2C, 2B, (A+B), (B+A), 2B, 2C, 2B, (A+B),(B+A), 2B, 2C, 2B, (A+B), (B+A), 2B, 2C
52	2A, 2E, 2A, 2B, 2A, 2G, 2G, 2A, 2B, 2A, 2E, 2E, 2A, 2B, 2A, 2E, 2E, 2A, 2B, 2A, 2G, 2G, 2A, 2B, 2A, 2E
53	2A, (B+A) 2B, 2B, (A+B), 2C, (B+A), 2B, 2B, (A+B), 2C, (B+A), 2B, 2B, (A+B) 2C, (B+A), 2B, 2B, (A+B), 2C, (B+A), 2B, 2B, (A+B), 2C
54	2A, (E+B), 2A, 2C, 2A, (B+G), (G+B), 2A, 2C, 2A, (B+E), (E+B), 2A, 2C, 2A, (B+E), (E+B), 2A, 2C, 2A, (B+G), (G+B), 2A, 2C, 2A, (B+E)
55	2A, 2A, (B+E), (E+B), 2A, 2C, 2A, (B+E), (E+B), 2A, 2C, 2A, (B+G), (G+B), 2A, 2C, 2A, (B+F), (F+B), 2A, 2C, 2A, (B+F), (F+B), 2A, 2C
56	2A, 2B, (A+B) 2C, (B+A), 2B, 2B, (A+B), 2C, (B+A), 2B, 2B, (A+B), 2C, (B+A), 2B, 2B, (A+B), 2C, (B+A), 2B, 2B, (A+B), 2C, (B+A), 2B
57	2A, 2A, 2E, 2E, 2A, 2B, 2A, 2E, 2E, 2A, 2B, 2A, 2G, 2G, 2A, 2B, 2A, 2E, 2E, 2A, 2B, 2A, 2E, 2E, 2A, 2B
58	2A, (B+A), 2B, 2C, 2B, (A+B), (B+A), 2B, 2C, 2B, (A+B), (B+A), 2B, 2C, 2B, (A+B), (B+A), 2B, 2C, 2B, (A+B), (B+A), 2B, 2C, 2B, (A+B)
59	2A, 2A, 2E, 2E, 2A, 2B, 2A, 2E, 2E, 2A, 2B, 2A, 2G, 2G, 2A, 2B, 2A, 2E, 2E, 2A, 2B, 2A, 2E, 2E, 2A, 2B
60	2A, 2A, (B+E), 2C, (E+B), 2A, 2A, (B+E), 2C, (E+B), 2A, 2A, (B+G), 2C, (G+B), 2A, 2A, (B+E), 2C, (E+B), 2A, 2A, (B+E), 2C, (E+B), (A+B)
61	2A, (A+B), (E+C), (C+E), (B+A), 2B, (A+B), (E+C), (C+E), (B+A), 2B, (A+B), (G+C), (C+G) (B+A), 2B, (A+B), (E+C), (C+E), (B+A), 2B, (A+B), (E+C), (C+E), (B+A), 2B
62	2A, 2A, 2E, 2E, 2E, 2A, 2A, 2E, 2E, 2E, 2A, 2A, 2G, 2E, 2G, 2A, 2A, 2E, 2E, 2E, 2A, 2A, 2E, 2E, 2E, 2A
63	2A, 2B, 2C, 2C, 2B, 2B, 2B, 2C, 2C, 2B, 2B, 2B, 2C, 2C, 2B, 2B, 2B, 2C, 2C, 2B, 2B, 2B, 2C, 2C, 2B, 2B

STEP	PICK UP
64	2A, 2A, (D+C), 2E, (C+D), 2A, 2A, (F+C), 2E, (C+F) 2A, 2A, (E+C), 2E, (C+E), 2A, 2A, (D+C), 2E, (C+D), 2A, 2A, (F+C) 2E, (C+F), 2A

65 As for 5, 66 as for 6, and so on, continue …

My table mat was made up of 229 rows and it is just slightly bigger than an A4 sheet of paper. A good place to stop is on row 44. Add 2 rows of background beads and finish up.

TO PUT IN A NEW THREAD, travel a little making a Z-pattern and then tug to make sure it won't slip. And continue. Always get rid of the old thread, *after* you have put in your new thread. Tidy at the end with travelling, never just cut.

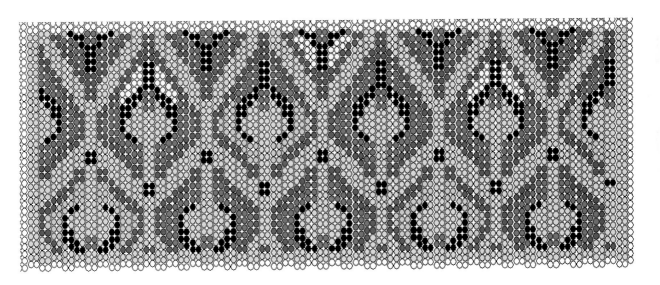

More Beadweaving Inspiration

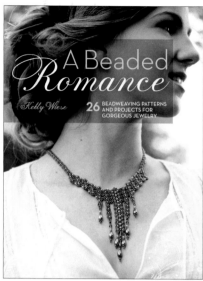

The Beaded Bracelet
Beadweaving Techniques
& Patterns for 20 Eye-Catching
Projects
Carole Rodgers

SRN: X9675
ISBN10: 144031277X

A Beaded Romance
26 Beadweaving Patterns and
Projects for Gorgeous Jewelry
Kelly Wiese

SRN: V8199
ISBN13: 9781440232138

Beaded Allure
Beadweaving Patterns for
25 Romantic Projects

SRN: Z4956
ISBN13: 9781600617683

Check out BeadingDaily.com—our vibrant, online beading community where you'll find free
beading projects, free beading stitch and jewelry making tutorials, expert advice, and information
about the latest trends in beading and jewelry making.